Unbreakable

Mangte Chungneijang Mary Kom is a boxer, a World Champion five times over and winner of an Olympic bronze medal in 2012 – the first time that women's boxing was part of the Olympic Games.

Praise for *Unbreakable*

'*Unbreakable* … should be made compulsory reading in every CBSE school. A real inspirational tale, it documents the struggles of Mary from being the daughter of a landless agricultural labour in Manipur struggling to make ends meet to five-time world and, finally, Olympic champion.'

– Boria Majumdar, *India Today*

'Mary's story is that classic story of winning against big odds. She doesn't talk about inspiration much, but her story is exactly that – an inspiration.'

– Shamya Dasgupta, *The Economic Times*

'This book is a read, not just for the sports aficionado … but for every woman, every youth, every child, every India. It's a remarkable story of a girl who came out of nowhere, stumbled her way through life, battled the odds … and came out triumphant.'

– Abraham C. Mathews, *Business World*

'Mary is a woman of refreshing candour. And her aptly-named autobiography … does full justice in bringing that out. It is an engaging read, filled with anecdotes and incidents – heart-wrenching and rib-tickling in equal measure – that traces her roller-coaster journey from being born in abject poverty to becoming one of India's most successful sportspersons.'

– Mihir Vasavda, *The Indian Express*

'What makes the book a winner is the short and crisp narration. The 140-page book is clear, to-the-point and full of action, much like her punches. Autobiographies, if not handled well, tend to turn into a rant, but there is not a single dull minute in her narrative.'

– womensweb.in

'*Unbreakable* is on the whole that rare kind of book – a truly worthy sports autobiography.'

– sportskeeda.com

Unbreakable
An Autobiography

MARY KOM

with

Dina Serto

Harper
Sport

An Imprint of HarperCollins *Publishers*

First published in India in 2013 by Harper Sport
An imprint of HarperCollins *Publishers*

Copyright © Mary Kom 2013

P-ISBN: 978-93-5116-009-0
E-ISBN: 978-93-5116-010-6

2 4 6 8 10 9 7 5 3

Mary Kom asserts the moral right
to be identified as the author of this work.

HarperCollins *Publishers*
A-75, Sector 57, Noida, Uttar Pradesh 201301, India
77-85 Fulham Palace Road, London W6 8JB, United Kingdom
Hazelton Lanes, 55 Avenue Road, Suite 2900, Toronto, Ontario M5R 3L2
and 1995 Markham Road, Scarborough, Ontario M1B 5M8, Canada
25 Ryde Road, Pymble, Sydney, NSW 2073, Australia
31 View Road, Glenfield, Auckland 10, New Zealand
10 East 53rd Street, New York NY 10022, USA

Typeset in Minion Pro 11/14
Jojy Philip, New Delhi 110 015

Printed and bound at
Thomson Press (India) Ltd.

Contents

Prologue

I live in Imphal, Manipur. My house, a government quarter in Langol Games Village, is only a couple of hours from Kangathei village, which is where I grew up. But when I think about it, I see what a long, long journey it has been for me, for all of us, from Kangathei to Imphal.

There are policemen standing outside the campus. They have big guns. It's a common sight everywhere in Manipur. Both the policemen and the army men.

Past them and through the tall gate is my home. As you enter, you'll see that the walls of my living room are full of framed photographs, photos that mark the milestones in my boxing career.

I never tire of them. In fact, every so often, I stop to look at them because I am never sure if all this is real – the Arjuna Award, the Padma Shri. Did I really get them? Here I am, standing next to President A.P.J. Abdul Kalam. There, the next president, Pratibha Devisingh Patil, is handing me the Rajiv Gandhi Khel Ratna award. There's a photograph of me with two former sports ministers, Uma Bharati and M.S. Gill. So many others. Photographs of me with people whom I couldn't have met – or did I?

These visual reminders root me to the present. They tell me that I will not wake up the next morning to find myself back in Kangathei, my family and I getting ready for another day of grinding labour in the fields.

As soon as I walk into the house, my twin sons come charging at me and right into my arms. They are quite a handful, always up to some mischief, and they are the centre of my life. Now, there is my third son. Yet another focus for my being. Onler – husband, friend, partner – smiles at this all-too-familiar scene.

My family: the surest reminder that I am here, that none of this is a dream.

My years of relentless labour, hard work, the refusal to give up, pushing every boundary I encountered. The thrill, the joy of fighting and winning, all my successes. Boxing, the sport I gave myself to. And the bronze medal from the 2012 London Olympics, my most prized possession. It is all real. All of it. I was the David who took on the Goliaths in the boxing ring – and I won, most of the time.

I thank God for making all of this possible.

1

And then I was born

My life has been a tough one, and my beginnings were extremely humble. But I don't wish for it to have been any different. At least in hindsight. Not at all. Because I realize that the hardships I faced in my formative years are the foundation of my strength. I am tough because of my background. They made me who I am today. They gave me the strength to keep fighting. Indeed, they made me want to fight in the first place.

I was born on 24 November 1982 in a village called Sagang in Manipur's Churachandpur district. Sagang is one of the biggest Kom villages, with more than a hundred families living there. I have no memory of the place, of course, because my family moved out when I was only five months old. Apa told me the story of why we left the village of our ancestors. It was also the story of why he became a landless farmer, despite being the descendant of a village chief.

His grandfather, my great grandfather, Khumneitong Mangte, was the chief of Sagang Khopui village. He was one of the greatest chiefs of his time. During the reign of Maharaj Churachand, he received a 'red shawl', presented only to chiefs who had earned the favour of the kings. To commemorate this event, Chief Mangte named his grandson, my father, 'Pontinkhup' ('pon' means cloth in the Kom language).

My father – his official name is Mangte Tonpa Kom – was born to Lerpu and Tonpi. My grandfather Lerpu, like his father, was a powerful and famed hunter. It's a skill he passed on to my father as well, who used to hunt for our food when I was a young child.

My grandfather, however, didn't become the next chief of the village. He was barely educated, and felt that a more learned and capable person ought to be the chief of such a big village. The times were changing, he said. So the chief's position passed to Singkhuplien Serto, who is the chief of Sagang to date. Grandfather was a farmer like everyone else in our village. He sent his son to a local Manipuri-medium school, but Apa soon stopped going to school so he could help his parents at home and on the farm. Life wasn't easy, finances even less so, and education was not going to put food on the table.

Apa had three brothers and two sisters. Over the years, as land was divided among the sons, sibling rivalries became sharper. The sons were careless in their tending of the land. The monsoons were irregular. Our family fell on hard times. The small farm my grandfather owned was not enough to feed his large family. Eventually, in 1971, Grandfather sent Apa off to the house of the chief of Kangathei, Moirang Akhup, to work as a farmhand. He was known to be one of the wealthiest men in the region and owned a lot of land. He always needed extra hands to help with the work. Chief Akhup's friends recommended Apa, who was young and was known to be honest, strong and hardworking.

And that's how my father began his life in Kangathei. He stayed in that village for more than ten years, working in the fields and doing any other chores that were asked of him. For my grandparents, it was one less mouth to feed, and it also meant constant help in terms of cash and rice, which the chief sent to their home.

So, although Apa was supposed to return home in two years, his stay at Akhup's was extended time and again. At a very young age, he learnt to fend for himself – a toughness I see in him to this day. Apa also decided that he would not marry because he didn't want to bring a wife and children into his world of abject poverty.

But God had other plans. On one of Father's rare visits home, grandfather, now old and ailing, asked him, 'When will I get to see my grandchild?' Father wondered about the question and the oddness of it – after all, grandfather was not starved of the sight of grandchildren. All his sons – except Apa and his youngest brother, Atorsing, still a child – were all married and had children. But the happiness of many children does not erase a parent's worry for any one child. Father did not want to disappoint his parents, and reconsidered the issue of marriage.

He had known my mother, Akham, in Kangathei for several years and felt that she would be a good match for him. They got married in 1981. Apa left Kangathei, and returned to Sagang and to his family.

Apa was an uneducated, landless labourer who found it hard to make ends meet. But in the midst of the struggle, in the ramshackle hut my parents lived in, I was born. Apa tells me that he was filled with happiness – both because he was holding his daughter and because he was able to fulfil Grandfather's wishes. Anu, on the other hand, was disappointed. Like most expecting mothers in India, she had hoped for a son. A daughter, she believed, would be more of a burden than a help. Would she be able to toil in the fields alongside her father as a son would? The disappointment was short-lived though, because she was soon wrapped in gratitude that her child was healthy, and in the happiness that she was now a mother.

The tradition in my tribe is to name the children after their elders. As a sign of respect to his mother-in-law, Apa chose to name me after her. So the first bit of my name would be 'Chung', after my grandmother Chungthem. I was named 'Chungneijang' – chung (high), nei (wealthy) and jang (agile). A prophetic name, or maybe just a name given by parents who had big hopes of their first child. The grandmother who christened me is still alive, although she's almost a hundred years old now – we can't be really sure of that, of course, because there were no written records in her day. She hardly recognizes me when I visit her these days. I give her money when I visit, and she holds it firmly, while asking for her favourite food items instead. She puts the money away because she wants to save it for her tombstone. I assure her each time that I will take care of that when the time comes. Every time I visit her, I notice that her memory has faded a little more.

A word here about Anu and her family. Unlike my father, Anu is big-built and tall. People who meet her tell me, 'Mary, if only you were like your mom, you could have been a better boxer.' Given my struggles with shifting to a higher weight category, I do sometimes feel it may have been easier for me if I were taller. But then again, I know now that experience matters more than height or weight.

Anu's parents were called Thangpu Leivon and, as I said,

Chungthem. She was named 'Saneikham', but is usually called just 'Akham'. Anu is one of seven children. Although my maternal grandparents were slightly better off than my father's family, they weren't rich, and could never help us financially.

To return to the story of my birth, it was a time when my parents had nothing to call their own. I was Apa's only proud possession. He called me 'sanahen', my eldest precious one. That's the endearment he uses to address me to this day.

As the family grew, so did the expenses, and this led to frequent feuds among the brothers. The atmosphere at home became increasingly unpleasant. Apa claimed his birthright – his share of grandfather's farmland. But the division of a small paddy field into four parts was far too painful a decision for grandfather to make. Instead, he told Apa:

> *Tonpa, cham mak jo roh,*
> *Inreng kho in ada lhon jo che*
> *Hoi Kho in angak jo che.*
>
> Tonpa, be anxious no more
> Hard times have abandoned you
> Good times lie in wait for you.

Of what use are words predicting good fortune to a man who has a wife and a baby to feed? Father considered other ways to earn a living; perhaps he could be a rickshaw driver in Imphal. But this would involve leaving us behind and living separately, which wasn't something he wanted to do if he could help it. Disappointed as he was at not getting his share of the land, Father decided to move back to Kangathei and leave Sagang forever. If he must live the life of a landless labourer, there was less ignominy in doing so away from his village. And Kangathei was the place he had spent his youth in. He had friends and well-wishers there. Above all, he could eke out a living without having to separate from his wife and daughter.

At Kangathei, we began from scratch. The village chief had given Apa land to build his own house. A thatched bamboo hut plastered with mud is a creation of skill and hard work – both of which my father had in abundance. It was in that house Apa built that I spent my childhood, learnt to handle household chores and began my education. It was there that my siblings, my sister Singlenei and brother Khupreng, were born soon after. It was there that my parents' struggle began in real earnest.

True to his word, except for the occasional family gathering, my father never returned. Grandfather has since passed away. I wish he were alive to remind Apa of his prophetic words.

2

All work and no play

Let me tell you a little about Kangathei, our adopted village. It is about two-and-a-half kilometres from Moirang, which is the nearest town. Moirang is significant for many reasons. It's close to the famous Loktak lake; it is a place of stories and folk tales and of much local history; it is where the Meiteis celebrate their famous Lai Haroaba festival; it is a meeting place for all the Koms from the neighbouring villages. It is where people gather to sell their vegetables and other produce, and where they go to buy household necessities. For all of these reasons, it is the place where people from different communities can meet and connect. They speak to each other in a dialect of Manipuri known as 'Meiteilon', which is why the tribal communities around Moirang are able to speak Manipuri (the language of the Meitei plains people) fluently – even if it is with an accent typical of the hill tribes.

Kangathei itself is a small village in the plains, surrounded by a vast expanse of rice fields. The road that leads to the village has been named Dr Kalam Road by the locals in honour of the then president's visit to Bunglon village (which it is also connected to) in 2006. Sadly, the road is in a state of utter disrepair now. But then again, most roads in Imphal are in a deplorable condition. They are riddled with potholes and, especially during the rainy season, there is frequent flooding due to clogged drains.

There is another marker to help the reader place my village, but it's a tragic one: it was the site of the Indian Airlines Boeing crash on 16 August 1991. The flight was coming in from Calcutta and veered into the nearby Thangjing Ching mountain range due to bad weather. Not one passenger survived. Kangathei was the base camp for the rescue operations that followed. Many locals, including my father, were hired to recover the bodies. To this day, the people of the area tell stories of the crash – embellished with ever wilder exaggerations as the years pass.

I was very young back then but I remember many people and many vehicles arriving. I remember that it rained, which was frustrating for the rescue workers. My father tells me that soon after the crash, the plane had been taken apart, and nothing was left behind, except the engine, which was probably too heavy to carry. There are many villages in the vicinity of the crash, and people frequent the hills to collect firewood and bamboo shoot and to hunt. They must have collected and sold the remnants of the airplane as scrap. I am told that the villagers made some very fine pots with that metal. Although I was only nine years old then, I remember that it happened on a Sunday, right after the church service. We heard a loud noise, and in no time, the village was full of policemen and other high officials. This was the first time I saw an aeroplane. I still remember with horror the sight of the bodies that were brought up close and kept in my village.

There were maybe twenty to twenty-five households in Kangathei. It was not a wealthy village. Because so few people had the opportunity to pursue higher education, hardly anyone worked in government departments. Anyone holding a government job, whatever the post, was held in high esteem. Most people in the village were farmers. Those with large paddy fields were considered rich. Landless farmers, like my father, had to work from morning to night just to feed their families. I remember that, after a whole day of hard work, like digging trenches, Apa earned just enough to buy rice for one day. When he could, he leased farms and cultivated rice. As a child, he had learnt how to hunt, fish and grow vegetables. When we had no money to buy rice, he would hunt and fish, and sell the fish to buy rice.

Rice is our staple food. Life in the village revolved around rice. The cycle begins in May to allow plantation in June or July and harvest in October or November. To be able to store rice for a whole year – that is every farmer's dream. During a good year, farmers manage to save enough for the year and end up with a little extra, which can be sold to pay for the children's education or for other household requirements. Every village celebrates a good harvest with a festival. From ancient times to this day, that hasn't changed.

To return to my own family; we were not one of the lucky ones with a year's stock of paddy and firewood. We had no farmland. And my parents had only a rudimentary education, that too in the local language. Convinced that his lack of education was at least partly to blame for his lot, Apa was determined that his children must go to an 'English school' and complete their matriculation. It was, of course, a dream way beyond his means: admission fees, monthly fees, textbooks, uniforms, the expenses were many. Still, it was something he was determined to provide for his children.

In the village, children go to school only when they are old enough to look after themselves, and that's at about six or seven years of age. In fact, they are by then old enough to look after others as well – the sight of a seven-year-old carrying a sibling on her back while her mother is busy with her work is not an unusual one. On the whole, kids have a lot of freedom in our society. They play in the open fields and wander around, and as long as they come home for meals, parents are not overly worried. My own childhood was a lot like that.

My first school was the Loktak Christian Model High School, run by a Presbyterian mission in Moirang. It was one of the town's best schools. My father had kept small sums of money aside from his meagre earnings so he could enrol me in a good school. And I remember how proud he was when he secured admission for me there.

In the Kom society of those days, boys were given preference when it came to education. Most people believed that, since a girl would get married and go away to her husband's home, there was little point in spending money educating them. But not my dad – he wanted his first-born to be the first in the family to pass class ten. Apa could have let me stay at home and then married me off early. Heaven knows he didn't have the wherewithal to do much more. But I am proud that he dared to think differently, and grateful for the farsightedness that has brought me so far.

My first day at school was a great occasion for the family. Anu put aside all work, pulled on her Sunday best and dropped me to school. She walked me to the classroom and left. I felt a bit awkward wearing a uniform and sitting amongst lots of children. But I didn't cry like the others, most of whom were younger than me and feeling equally lost. Soon enough, I had made friends. I remember Ranjita and Sophiya, in whose company I spent my early school days. School and studies gradually became a part of my routine.

I used to walk to school every day – a one-hour trek one way into town. I remember vaguely that Mother accompanied me for a few months, and then I was left to go on my own with friends from the village. This was by no means unusual. Parents in the villages are far too busy with their hard physical labour to mollycoddle their children. Anu would come to school only to pay my fees every month. When my sister and brother started school, it was my responsibility to care for them in school as well as at home.

It wasn't that all children in the village worked as hard as we did. Many of my friends spent their time playing, eating and sleeping, even though some of their families were as poor as ours. But Father had trained us to work from a young age. There were many jobs I could do that even the boys struggled with. All three of us siblings were given our chores, and as the eldest, I took my responsibilities very seriously. I helped in the fields, even with ploughing the fields – a task that required immense strength, because the bullocks were not easy to control. The menfolk would stand and gape, seeing me drive the animals.

There were leeches in the wet rice fields, even the occasional water snakes. The leeches I'd pull off with my hands, and a well-aimed stone would knock out the snakes. Many years later, when I was training at a boxing camp, my friends spotted a snake, screamed and ran away. I ran after the snake and knocked it out with just one kick. Seeing that, the others came running and killed it with sticks.

Apart from ploughing, work in the fields required handling heavy farming tools, carrying bundles of rice saplings for planting and later, sacks of rice. I would carry home the straw that was left over after harvesting, to store as cattle-feed. That aside, I would carry water across long distances, because we had no potable water in the village. I went up the hills with Apa to collect firewood and to the lake to fish. I was Apa's right-hand woman, but Anu needed me to help too. Cooking, washing clothes, gardening, cleaning the house and various other odd jobs – that was also part of my routine.

I was the older child and the one that both my parents leant on. Even now, if you ask my mother, she'll tell you I was an obedient child. But as I tended to our cows and ensured they were feeding well – they were our most prized possessions – I would look into the distance, where children were playing in the village grounds. I was envious, I admit. Which child wouldn't be? But looking back, it was that sustained toil that prepared my body for boxing. My strength and stamina continue to be my strong points even when I fight bigger opponents in the ring.

Through those years, though, there was no time for regrets or complaints. My parents worked harder than anyone we knew and made endless sacrifices. Apa, for instance, was the village wrestling champion in his youth. But, with a wife and children to support, he had no time for that sort of leisure. Anu, too, spent all her waking hours working: weaving, gardening, helping in the fields. She sold the shawls she wove to pay our school fees. All our vegetables came from her kitchen garden, and whatever was left over was sold in the market.

It's another matter that, at the end of all this, we could

not always pay our school fees on time – something that embarrassed us greatly. We were not allowed to enter the classroom or sit for exams when this happened. Anu tried her best to save us these unpleasant experiences, saving and scrimping as much as she could. God-fearing and hard-working, my mother is the strongest person I know.

Anu remembers me as an undemanding child. She says that I understood we were hard-up. Our big celebration in the year was Christmas. For many of us, it was the only time we got new clothes to wear. Anu says that while I always accepted what was bought for me without fuss, and did not ask for more, I preferred boyish clothes, like jeans or shorts and T-shirts, to frocks.

There was one thing my siblings and I could not make our peace with. My father would sometimes leave home at the break of dawn to go hunting and fishing. Anu packed the day's food for him, for he returned only after dark. We crowded around him excitedly then, waiting to see the catch of the day. He was an expert at catching eels, which my parents would spread out in the kitchen. The big ones were exchanged for rice in the village. Much later, Anu told me how much it hurt her when the three of us would innocently ask why all the big fish were being sent away, leaving only the small ones for us. Of course, only the big fish fetched a decent price. Apa still has a passion for fishing, except now he brings home only enough for a meal or so – and he always ensures that the biggest ones are sent to me.

Apa was also an ace marksman. He claims that he has shot a hundred birds with hundred pellets of an air gun. Because he was such a skilled hunter, there was always smoked fish and meat hanging above the fireplace at home. We were poor, but we did not eat poorly. In later years, when I left home for training, Anu would pack some of that smoked meat for me, because it preserved well. It certainly lifted some of the weight, the sadness of being away from home.

For all the fishing, hunting and farming Apa did, and all the weaving and gardening Anu did, they did not always have enough to feed and educate three children. So there were times when Apa left home for months in search of work, usually to work as a woodcutter in the jungles of Ukhrul or Tamenglong, more than a hundred kilometres from home. There, he hired himself out as a contract labourer. The mahajans only paid after the work was completed, which often took two or three months at a stretch. Deep inside the forest, the workers cut trees and then carried them long distances manually and stockpiled them on the road for transportation.

Apa says that there was only one truck that could drive up those rugged hills, the Shaktiman. The woodcutters had to wait for the truck to arrive, then load the wood on it, travel with it to the nearest town and return to the forest. He also remembers several near-death experiences from those days. Once, while cutting wood, he fell from a high tree on to a thorn bush. He had cuts and bruises from the thorns that pierced his skin. There was no medication or treatment available deep in the jungle, so he just pulled out the thorns himself and waited for the wounds to heal on their own. Many a time, he spent days alone in the forest. When he slept at night, it was always in a half-sitting position, so if an animal were to attack, he would be able to get up and escape quickly. His small, tough frame has endured a lot. When we talk of those times now, he has tears in his eyes. Is he happy or sad? A bit of both, he says. 'I'm sad about the hard times, happy that you're so successful today.'

Night falls early in the east, just as dawn arrives early. It is only after dinner, when it's pitch black outside and not conducive to work, that my parents sit down and relax. There was no television in the village then; we certainly couldn't afford one. So Apa would ask me to roll out the mat and study. I would be bone-tired, but this was the only time I could catch up on homework and other assignments. I would sit down on the mat and pull a boton close to me. Candles were expensive, so we used these kerosene lamps made from used bottles and cotton wicks. They emitted a lot of smoke and only a very dim light.

One boton was enough for our entire house, which was just one room, with an attached kitchen. It was made of bamboo, plastered with a mix of mud, cow dung and straw, and covered with a thatched roof. In it were two beds – one for my sister and me, another for my parents and brother – with mattresses made of straw mixed with a little locally grown cotton. We would sew pieces of cloth together to make blankets. Neither our clothes, nor the blankets actually kept us warm. Winters were bitterly difficult. There was a string to hang clothes from and a trunk in which we stored our Sunday clothes. Apa loved to tell the story of how he had saved money in his youth to buy a fine mattress made with the best local cotton. He lost it and though he does have an idea about who might have taken it, he does not want to make an issue of it. That sort of luxury was well beyond reach in his life as a family man.

I would do my homework as fast as I could, read a lesson or two and then get ready for bed. The moment my head touched the pillow, I'd fall asleep. In the morning, Apa called out, 'Wake up, Sanahen, you have to help me before school.' How I longed to sleep just a little longer. But I always jumped out of the bed and got ready for the day. It was still dark outside while I washed up. All ready, I started the fire with a few dried twigs and boiled water in one of our few battered pots and pans. Father and I had a cup of tea and set out. He reminded me when it was time for school. I'd rush back home, eat a hurried lunch and set off.

My day used to be a rush all the way through. My feet were fast, but my hands were even faster, trying to cope with work at home and at school.

By the time I set out for school, my friends were already on their way there. I'd run and catch up with them. They'd say to me, 'Chungneijang, you run like the wind.' The only shoes my parents could afford were made of rubber, and they would wear out quickly because of my long trek to school. But Anu became an expert at repairing them by heating iron tongs and pressing them together on the tear to join the pieces. By the time school term was over, the rubber shoes were ready to fall to pieces.

I didn't care that my shoes were patched up, or that my uniform was crushed. For me, school was a chance to play with friends and learn things that my parents couldn't teach me. Still, I was a mediocre student. Every day, mother would give me 50 paise as tiffin money, with which I bought small packets of dried fruits, channa and Moreh pickles. At home, the only food available was whatever was left over from the day's lunch. Sometimes not even that. During the season, I would climb a guava tree that grew behind the old church and eat my fill of ripe guavas after school. In fact, my family and I often quelled our hunger with the seasonal fruits that grew in the village.

The church held a special significance in our lives. Although my parents worked hard through the week, they rested on Sundays. It was a day spent in church and prayer, and relaxing with the family. I belong to the Baptist church, and have grown up with the strong conviction that God will answer my prayers. In spite of our penury and deprivation, we did not ever lose faith in God. If anything, God was the force that kept us going, fighting and hoping for better times. The Biblical story of David and Goliath has been a constant inspiration for me – an identification deepened by my own diminutive size. I have clear memories from my childhood, of going to church every single Sunday, reading the Bible, listening to the priest, singing endless choruses and songs. To this day I fast and pray on a Sunday before any major championship, no matter where in the world I am.

The other thing I remember about those days is that there were not that many avenues for entertainment in the village. Only a very few families could afford a television. My family could afford one only after I got my first prize money in 2002. But we would watch movies at my uncle's house sometimes. My favourite movies were the action-packed martial art films starring Bruce Lee, Jet Li and Jackie Chan. Hindi films were boring. We didn't understand the language, and after the blanket ban by militant groups on Hindi films in 2000, they weren't available anyway.

When anyone in the village happened to acquire a new video cassette, news of it travelled very quickly. We all visited the home with the cassette and packed into a room to watch the movie. Afterwards all of us kids would imitate the hero and aim kicks at each other. I wanted to be a fighter like those martial arts heroes and my cousin Chungjalen was the usual recipient of my Bruce Lee kicks. He and I were the eldest in our families and shared many good and bad times. As we tended cows or worked in the fields together the two of us would discuss our dreams of becoming rich and helping our parents.

Holidays weren't entertainment time either. Since my siblings and I were free from school, father would assign us other work and errands, like collecting firewood. Since we couldn't afford to stockpile firewood, like most other families, we had to pick up bits and pieces of leftover firewood. Apa and the three of us kids would troop off to Ningthi Ching hills, about eight kilometres from our village. He would climb high up and leave us waiting at the foothills to catch the firewood he threw down the slope. By evening we'd have quite a bit and we'd walk all that distance back with the load on our heads. Once Apa and I had gone to collect firewood by ourselves. He was high up on a hill and I was waiting further down, holding on to a plant to keep from falling down. But the plant came right out of off the ground and I went hurtling down into a hole. I blacked out. When I came to, I was lying flat on my face, hands and legs bruised. When Apa came down, I showed him my injuries. He felt terrible and checked to make sure that no bones were broken. We set off for home after resting awhile. All of this no doubt inured me to the cuts and bruises I would endure in the course of my boxing life.

Perhaps I sound like my childhood was a dreary one, filled with no play and no joy. It wasn't like that. In the midst of all the work, there were times I'd sneak out to play with friends. I was a champion marble player with a very sharp strike and usually ended up winning all of my friends' marbles. Sometimes I sold them their own marbles, at other times I lent them some so we could continue playing. I often ended up playing against grown men who wanted to test my skills. I seldom played with the girls. I was rough and tough and was constantly looking to feed my fighting spirit. I was also a bad loser who would do anything to win a game. That at least has not changed. For me, a competition is meant to be won.

One day, I was playing marbles outside the house when my brother came to inform me that Anu had sent for me. I ignored him, and he kept his distance because he didn't trust my temper. Mother had him call me again, and then a third time. I was in a bad mood already because I was losing. As soon as he came near me, I turned around and kicked him with such force that he had to be taken to the hospital. Fortunately, there was no serious injury, but I was terribly sorry. My brother and sister looked up to me. I was more like an elder brother than a sister to them. If anyone bullied them, they would have me to answer to. Once my brother came home crying because a bully had beaten him up. My brother pointed out the boy to me, and I went and twisted his ears so hard, he apologized and promised never to repeat his offence.

But there was another time when my brother was responsible for sending me to the hospital. We were playing hide-and-seek, and he was hiding behind a door. I didn't know that and peeped through the keyhole. Suddenly, he poked a stick through it. Fortunately, it hit the white of the eye and caused no severe injury. With a bandage over my eye, I happily set off to play marbles with my friends – it was perfect for taking aim.

I always looked forward to the annual games and sports meet in school, and competed in practically every individual sporting event: 100 metres, 400 metres, long-distance and so on. Then there were the less serious events, like the spoon race (in which we ran the race with a spoon in our mouths, careful not to drop the marble balanced on it) and the needle race (run, thread a needle, run back). I bagged the first prize in most events I participated in. The prizes were household items like plates, cups and tiffin boxes, much to my family's delight. My brother was very excited about the tiffin box, because now he could take rice to school like his friends did.

As my focus moved to sports, my academic performance started sliding. Father was very distressed by this. He wanted his children to never have to face the discrimination and disadvantages that his own lack of education forced him to bear with. He did not want me to waste my time playing.

But we had more immediate concerns. Back in those days, pocket money was an unheard-of concept, but my friends and I found ways to make small amounts. We would collect tins, containers and bottles and sell them to the hawker who collected and sold these things. One time, we went off to glean rice in the harvested fields of the rich landowners – something that poor people did to collect rice. At the end of a day's careful picking, grain by grain, we had but a small basket of rice, which we sold. Every now and then my brother ribs me about the fact that I am yet to give him his share of that money! At other times, I picked wild vegetables and fruits and sold them. With this money, I would buy textbooks, pencils, erasers and so on. Sometimes Anu would borrow money from me, and then I would remind her repeatedly to return it till she did.

After my class six exams, I was shifted to St Xavier's School, also in Moirang. I don't remember why I made the move. My brother was at Xavier's, and perhaps my parents wanted us to be in the same school. The best thing about the new school was its huge playground. At the new school too, I continued to participate and excel in all individual sports. So much so that my principal and teachers suggested that I should consider a career in sports. One day, the principal summoned Apa and suggested that he take me to the Sports Authority of India (SAI) in Imphal. This worried my father more than it pleased him. Where was he to find the resources to send his daughter to Imphal? He decided not to think about it just yet.

But I still have my own little sporting memories from the time. The most vivid of those is the annual meet of the Kom-Rem Students' Union at Thayong village in 1998. It was a gathering of Kom youth from all over Manipur. My parents tried to dissuade me from going. Perhaps they were worried about the expenses. But when I insisted they relented, and my friends and I set out. I travelled on the roof of a bus with the boys throughout the eight-kilometre journey. I was happy and excited. Sitting at that height, a bright scarf around my head, I felt on top of the world. Nothing that followed – my first train ride, my first flight, my first visit abroad – ever matched the sheer delight of that childhood journey. We reached in the evening and I was amazed at the beauty of the village and the scenery. I seem to remember someone telling me that Thayong is famous for its juicy pineapples. At the meet I participated in all the athletic events and outshone the others easily. I made friends as well as quite a name for myself in the community.

But back in the village life continued as before – except that Apa had saved enough money by then to buy me a Captain bicycle. I would ride with my friends, my sister usually perched on the carrier at the back. One day I pedalled so fast that my sister fell off. I heard my friends yelling at me to stop and turned back to find the carrier empty. I had to cycle back quite a distance to pick her up. My friends and I would often race to school and I would beat boys even bigger than I was. I used to pretend I was riding a motorcycle, like some of the boys zooming past us.

3

Playing too was hard work

As the days and months passed, Apa gradually began to accept my fierce passion for sport. He began enquiring about the best options available, so he could send me for further training. He wanted to find a way to indulge me without disturbing my school and studies.

He took me to Nipamacha Kunam, a National Institute of Sports (NIS)-trained coach, at Moirang. Oja Nipamacha was an athletics coach and had nurtured many youngsters. I was thrilled when he accepted me as his student. 'Will you come early in the morning for exercises and training?' he asked me sternly. I assured him I would do my best. There was no admission fee to this course, nor were there equipment charges. All I had to do was show up and train alongside the other athletes. The only concern was that I did not have a balanced diet to support my training.

Sure enough, the strain of cycling between Moirang and my village four times every day became too much. It was also clear to me that athletics was not my cup of tea. In about twenty days I gave up. Still, there was a lot I learnt in that short stint, most crucially, the right techniques of exercise. I learnt stretching, exercises to build strength, stamina and speed training. We did a lot of running as well. My first coach commended me on my skills and told me I needed proper guidance to hone my talent. Even after I stopped going to the centre I kept up the exercise routine at home, hoping that another opportunity would crop up. Sometimes I wonder how I sustained my passion given that I had neither exposure to the possibilities nor opportunities.

As people around me – teachers and friends – began to speak about my talent for sports, and as my zeal continued unabated, Apa's acceptance of my sporting ambitions deepened. He began to consider the idea that my future lay in sports and not academics. He contacted relatives in Imphal so I could stay with them if I got an opportunity to develop my talents in that city, the capital of Manipur, the place where I had the best chance of learning and training. Though, at this stage, I really didn't have any idea about which sport I was going to pursue. Boxing? No, that wasn't even in my thoughts.

Apa began making enquiries about the SAI facility in Imphal. I was over the moon. In spite of my limited exposure, I knew that SAI was the place with the best sporting facilities. We had visited Imphal on a school excursion in the late '90s. I remember that the Khuman Lampak Sports Stadium was then under construction for the upcoming National Games. Promptly, I began to make plans for the future. I would pursue a career in sports and get a job under the sports quota, and then I would help my parents so they'd no longer be poor. Jobs are scarce in Manipur and I had heard it said that the only way to get one was either through political connections or with money, paying bribes. Never in a million years would my parents save enough to buy me a job. But the sports quota was another way in. Once he had accepted my dream, Apa took on my share of the work as well so that I would have more time to play.

I was about sixteen when Apa finally let me have my way and focus on sports. He had tried to dissuade me over and again. He knew that poverty would not allow him to provide me with the kind of diet, equipment, clothes or money that I would need. He was hurt by the thought that my friends would think me pitiable. He never did speak about the possibility that I might get a job through the sports quota, but I knew about it, even if the details of how it worked were hazy to me back then. Yet I persisted.

The fact is that I was never interested in the pursuits of girls around me. Most of my friends were boys – although that was partly because there were very few girls of my age in the village. I was energetic and restless. Also, quite frankly, neither my parents nor I thought I was particularly good-looking. If anything, I was rather self-conscious about my boyish appearance and the fact that feminine clothes didn't look good on me. In all sorts of ways, sports always seemed like the way forward to me.

Apa may not have been educated but he knew about life, and was keen to share with his children all that he knew. He would say to me, 'Sanahen, being a woman, you should be able to do everything.' Or 'Don't tell lies. Be good and kind-hearted. Treat your elders with love and care.' So I strove to learn how to run a home, and cook and clean – even as I learnt to work alongside him and play alongside my peers.

The most significant lesson I learnt was one Apa taught me: of the dignity of hard labour and honesty.

Nangna touba, nangna phangba
Eina touba, eina phangba.

What you sow, you will reap
What I sow, I will reap.

Those were words I took with me to Imphal in 1999, when I left to try and get a seat at SAI. Anu and I set off for the city together. As the bus started moving, I felt a pang of sadness and worry at leaving my home behind. I was worried about my siblings. I wondered if I was being selfish, with my parents now having to do all the work, even the share I took care of. What would my siblings do? Now my parents would have to handle them as well.

But I also felt that I was making the right move. We went to the home of Anu's nephew, Chungthang, who was working with the Life Insurance Corporation. Mother explained to him that I was moving to the city to pursue a career in sport. I remember with gratitude his warmth and hospitality. Chungthang telephoned a colleague, who in turn helped us meet Coach Gosana at SAI Takyel. It seems surprising to me when I think about it now. But I really went to Imphal to try my luck, without admission. Fortunately, the coach was impressed by my determination and agreed to train me until it was time for the formal selection to be done. Chungthang advised me to choose an individual sport, saying that it would have more scope. He also helped me get admission in Adimjati Government High School in Class IX. I hadn't had the benefit of many advisors and took my cousin's words seriously. As it turned out, he was right, for my inclination was towards individual sport.

My school was quite a distance from SAI. I would wake up at 4 a.m. and cycle to the Academy, return at 8 a.m., and then head to school. This was particularly tough during Manipur's cold winter days. But I was not the only one. There were many youngsters on the road, cycling and jogging on their way to their respective sports complexes.

I spent the next two years shuttling between the houses of various relatives and friends as I juggled my training and academic schedules. Mornings were the busiest, of course, and evenings were when I caught up with school work and my books. My parents visited me sometimes, bringing dried fish and meat. While my hosts were all very good to me, I felt that my tight schedule and unusual hours were an imposition on them. About two years after I moved to Imphal, I rented an affordable house with some friends.

The house was not very far from the training centre. I cooked my own meals there – more often than not, just one meal, because I was so absorbed in my training. L. Sarita Devi was one of the girls who stayed with me. Generally, we were all quite busy, so there wasn't the sort of time to socialize with friends as there might be in a girls' hostel. I preferred to do my own cooking and provide for myself, which also ensured that I could live within my own budget. After some time, Sarita moved out but I stayed on, because the rent was cheap and about as much as I could afford.

One day I noticed that my stock of rice was over. There was a bandh the next day. Bandhs and blockades are frequent occurrences in Manipur, politically sensitive and disturbed as the region is. I had no money. Reluctant to borrow from friends, I cycled four hours to Kangathei and brought back rice. It wasn't easy living alone in a rented house on next to nothing, but it did give me the freedom to concentrate on my sport. My drive to succeed was so strong that it drove away all fear and apprehension.

During my stay at SAI I tried my hand at a number of different things: pole vault, javelin throw and various track and field sports. The coaches at the Academy wanted to see what worked best for me. They felt that I might be suited for gymnastics but I thought I was probably too old to be starting out in a sport that girls take up when they are really small and more flexible. The truth is also that none of these sports really appealed to me. I wanted something like the martial arts, something with a lot of action. Unfortunately, SAI Takyel mostly catered to track and field disciplines. I realized very soon that I should leave before the formal selection for athletes was done.

I had joined SAI as an outsider – by which I mean, just on the basis of an understanding between the coach and me – so there was no strict rule about leaving. Though I did feel guilty about leaving without speaking to Oja Gosana.

At about that time there was talk that women's boxing might be introduced at SAI. I was very excited. The idea of boxing appealed to me immensely. During the National Games in 1999 at Khuman Lampak, there had been an exhibition bout by senior women boxers L. Sarita Devi and Sandhyarani Devi. Sadly, I wasn't able to go see the matches. Then came the news that Dingko Singh, a Manipuri, had won the gold in the 1998 Bangkok Asian Games, which led to a greater buzz around boxing in the state. He was our newest icon. Although I had never seen Dingko, I secretly wished to be like him. Talk was that Dingko had won that gold after having been dropped from the national team and then reinstated again. He was not a hero only to me, but to all of Manipur.

Apart from Dingko, my other childhood icons were Muhammad Ali and his daughter Laila Ali.

But it was a chance meeting with Rebika Chiru, a boxer, that really set me on the right path. This was back in the days when I was still staying at Chungthang's home on K.R. Lane. Rebika would often walk past the house wearing a National Games tracksuit. I learnt that she was a boxer and arranged for my friends to introduce us. She told me that women's boxing had already been introduced at SAI Khuman Lampak, and that she was among a handful of women training there. By this time, I had made up my mind that boxing was the sport I was looking for.

I started enquiring about admission to the Academy's course. I found out that the chief coach, L. Ibomcha Singh, was one of the best boxing coaches at SAI. So I set off all by myself to meet him. A National Boxing Champion in 1986, who had won the bronze at Pune, he had also been selected to represent India at the President's Cup in Jakarta that year. But he was dropped at the last minute for reasons I don't know. Frustrated and disappointed, he packed his bags, returned to Manipur and threw himself into training students. He has produced many outstanding boxers – men and women – from Manipur over the years.

I did not know back then that Oja Ibomcha was very particular about his training schedule. He did not talk to visitors, entertain phone calls or speak to parents during those hours. I had no idea what he looked like even. I walked into the hall. There were many students milling around. I enquired of several of them, 'Who is Oja Ibomcha?' Then a big, beefy man who looked like a Manipuri Mike Tyson walked up to me and said, 'I am Sir Ibomcha. What do you want with me?' I told him right away that I wanted him to coach me. He was taken aback at my boldness but I also aroused his curiosity. He asked me where I was from, who I was and who had sent me. To that last, I answered that Oja Gosana from SAI had sent me. Of course this wasn't true. I just blurted it out because I was intimidated. Truth be told, I had left Oja Gosana's camp without even informing him. Ibomcha asked me to wait outside, saying that he didn't like to be disturbed in the middle of a training session.

I sat outside, praying hard to God that everything should work out well. I was practically in tears.

Finally, Oja Ibomcha came out and called me over. 'Why do you want to join boxing?' That day, I was wearing a gold earring my mother had bought for me with her kitty money. 'You are a small, frail girl. With your gold earring, you don't even look like a boxer. Boxing is for young boys.' I must have looked devastated at this, for he quickly asked me about my parents, what they did and where I was staying in Imphal. He was worried that if I was staying in a village far away, I wouldn't be able to maintain his strict training schedule: 6–9 a.m. and 3–6 p.m. His parting shot was, 'If you're really interested, you may join, but I am very strict about the routine and timing. If you can't keep up, don't join.'

I went away ecstatic. Finally, I would follow my dream. I did not, however, stay in the hostel. Selections for the hostel were done through physical tests and performance-based evaluations by coaches.

A few days later, I began training. Oja Ibomcha was a hard taskmaster. But the rigorous exercises and training did not dull my enthusiasm one bit. I learnt fast. I came to realize that I was a born boxer, with a natural, inborn style. All I needed to do was train and perfect my footwork and punches. My life so far had prepared me for the endurance training that is so essential to boxing, but not the specific skills that boxers need. That's what I had to learn and that's what I focused on.

In fact, every now and then, I overworked myself, not knowing that it would have an adverse effect on my health. All I wanted to do was prove that being young, a girl and small-statured would not keep me back. More than once, Oja Ibomcha scolded me for training when the others were doing social work – cleaning the gym, the boxing hall and the yard outside the SAI campus. The extra activity was supposed to help us learn cooperation and friendliness. But my obsession with boxing was such that I didn't want to waste time doing anything else. I thought the occasional admonishments were well worth the time I spent practising. I was too young to understand the adverse effects it might have in the long run. Fortunately, I had my coach looking out for me.

We had to follow a weekly schedule of different exercises to remain fit. The schedule was divided into morning and afternoon sessions of three hours each.

Monday
| MORNING | Fitness exercises |
| EVENING | Playing, tactics and training |

Tuesday
| MORNING | Technique |
| EVENING | Control sparring tactics |

Wednesday
| MORNING | Speed endurance, which is a vital part of stamina-building |

EVENING   Recreational games, to expose athletes to sports other than boxing; entertainment programmes like singing or talent shows were organized. (These extra-curricular activities helped us de-stress. Since singing is very much a part of our culture, I am happy to oblige when asked to sing, with a Manipuri song or a popular Hindi film song.)

Thursday

MORNING   Circuit training to improve mobility, strength and stamina.

EVENING   Tactics training.

Friday

MORNING   Conditioning and fitness training, to build and strengthen body parts according to the needs of each player.

EVENING   Sparring sessions organized in competition-like bouts, which enabled us to display the tactics we had learnt.

Saturday

MORNING   Long endurance, especially running, to build stamina and strength. This is very important for boxers. Other field training exercises were also assigned to us as part of long endurance training.

EVENING   Social work, which meant cleaning the boxing hall and campus. This was done to instil a feeling of cooperation and team spirit among us.

Sundays were holidays. I would go to church and spend the rest of the day visiting friends, eating at roadside eateries with them or riding around on a borrowed two-wheeler.

This was the regimen I followed for most of my early years in boxing. Following a systematic, well-balanced routine prepared my raw talent for the rigours of the sport. I also gathered that the best way to defeat an opponent was to be fast and furious. My coaches down the years also appeared to agree that intimidating the opponent early on is good strategy.

I learnt all I could from Oja Ibomcha, and he remains one of my best coaches ever. The Government of India recognized his contribution to the field of boxing by giving him the Dronacharya Award in 2010.

I was a novice in the boxing world back then. It was only later that I learnt about the unspoken rivalry between Manipur's various boxing circles. The state-run Youth Affairs and Sports (YAS) boxing academy was run by coach Narjit Singh, while Khoibi Salam was the secretary of the Manipur Amateur Boxing Association (MABA), of which Oja Kishan was the coach. I soon discovered that there was a nexus between YAS and MABA, as a result of which students from SAI were often dropped during selections. There was also talk that SAI students may not be allowed to participate in state-level tournaments.

I didn't want to take any chances, so I decided to leave SAI in order to qualify for the state-level tournament in May 2000. Oja Ibomcha knew how things worked and did not object when his students moved out of SAI. I had been boxing for a little over a month when I shifted to the state coaching facility. But after the competition, I came back to Ibomcha, as did several other boxers. This came to be something of a pattern.

After leaving SAI, I approached Oja Narjit. He accepted me, and I trained for a few weeks under him. He was very dedicated to his work. Women's boxing was a new department back then, with practically no facilities to support it. But the coach was enthusiastic and the girls were passionate, and so we managed without proper infrastructure. Most of us had come from places outside Imphal, and were struggling to find good, safe accommodation. Oja Narjit arranged for us to stay on campus at Khuman Lampak in one of the office building rooms. He personally came to check on us to ensure that we were safe. To us, he was both coach and guardian. His motto was: discipline, dedication, determination. Today, with only a few years left before his superannuation, Oja Narjit still coaches his students in an open ring with just a roof over it. He hopes that the Ministry of Sports will upgrade the boxing arena in Khuman Lampak during his tenure.

Later, I shifted to MABA under Coach L. Kishan Singh, who ran a boxing club known as KYDC, or the Konjung–Hazari Youth Development Committee Club, which I represented in my first appearance as a boxer. Oja Kishan was the youngest of my coaches, and a dedicated and hard-working teacher. Working with him, I honed the basics that I had learnt under Oja Ibomcha.

A few seniors had already been training at KYDC for about two years. Sarita was there, as were Sandhyarani, Th. Joymati and N. Asharani. I was excited and confident right from the start. Since most of the girls were from a higher weight category, I practised with Sushila Devi and Bibi, the only two from my category. My sparring partners tended to be junior boys in the 40–45 kg category. My punches were too much for the girls, so I had no choice but to spar with the boys, who were of my height but younger. I matched their strength and stamina in boxing hits.

In just three months, I had trained under three coaches. All of these coaches enriched my game and my insight into it. They must have done something right, for in my very first State Championships, I defeated Humbi in the finals; she had been one of my coaches when I first started boxing at SAI.

It remains a pretty contentious matter, the question of who began and propelled women's boxing in Manipur. The various sports departments – YAS, MABA and SAI – all vied for credit. The fact is that at that time, a number of factors came together, and all these organizations and various people within them contributed to producing world-class boxers, both male and female, in Manipur. Dingko Singh, and later Suranjoy Singh, Nanao Singh and Devendro Singh among the men, and Sarita, Sandhyarani, Mandakini Chanu, Sarjubala Devi and I among the women, have won various national and international championships. All of us stepped into the world of boxing under the guidance of the state's coaches.

The Indian Amateur Boxing Federation (IABF), with permission from AIBA, the governing body of the sport, gave the green signal for the introduction of women's boxing in 1998, but in Manipur, coaches had been enrolling and training women enthusiastically since 1996. The sport became more popular after the exhibition bout at the 1999 National Games in Khuman Lampak, which I could not make it to. Several girls from Manipur, including Sandhyarani, Sarita and Geeta Chanu featured in the exhibition matches. That the Manipur Boxing Association (MBA), under the guidance of Khoibi Salam, took the lead in introducing the sport before any other state in the country is admirable though not surprising, given that it is women who contribute the most to household finances in Manipur. They work both inside and outside the home. In sport too, then, women find opportunities and encouragement in the state.

This early start is in good measure responsible for how well women boxers from Manipur have done in competitions. Between 2000 and 2006, Manipur dominated women's boxing. But now, states like Haryana, which have more resources, are entering the fray seriously and doing very well.

That said, as far as coaches go, Manipur has been particularly fortunate. Oja Ibomcha has been working at SAI, teaching the many students he has taken under his wing, with dedication and enthusiasm. Oja Narjit at YAS had begun boxing while in the army, a job he left so he could teach boxing. At the MBA, the secretary, Khoibi Salam, and Oja Kishan have handled the selection and coaching of boxers. Oja Kishan also trains students in his own house, even though there is no boxing ring or gym there. I was one of his early students (just before the May 2000 tournament), and I remember that he commended me saying, 'She performs even better than what she's taught.' I remember, too, that a group of women boxers and I stayed in his house for some time, until we could find accommodation close by. The coaches, every one of them, spared no effort. They were also sensitive to the fact that most of us were from low-income families and far-flung areas and villages. We often had to travel great distances to reach the training venue. At times we could not make it to the venue because we just did not have enough bus fare. Through all of this, our coaches were understanding, less strict than we thought they would be. (Although this was not always the case for those selected to SAI; Oja Ibomcha was known to be very strict.)

As inspiring as our coaches were, I picked up early on that there was a system to be negotiated. That I had to be at the right place at the right time. The rules as they stood gave MBA the power to select boxers, which meant that the athletes coached by the state coach were the ones who were eligible for selection to the state team. This has been a constant source of conflict between MBA and SAI. With its resources coming from the Centre, SAI has better infrastructure, boxing equipment and hostel facilities. So students often shift to SAI to train there. But when it's time for selection they have no choice but to go back to the State Boxing Centre.

Not only does this rule inconvenience players, it creates a highly avoidable rift among the coaches. Groupism and favouritism are the inevitable consequences of it. The boxing community in Manipur is like two war camps, ever in readiness to fight one another. I shuttled between them to ensure that I kept both happy. I was interested only in furthering my sporting career and could have done without this sort of unpleasantness. I do not doubt for a moment the sincerity of our coaches. They were committed to producing very good players but every coach wanted the entire credit for himself. The atmosphere among the students was one of insecurity. If I train at SAI my chances of getting to the Nationals are low. If I train only at the state coaching centre my performance tends to go down because SAI has better coaches and better facilities. If the MBA and SAI joined hands they would turn out many more world-class boxers than the handful that have managed to navigate the system.

I single-handedly fought my way through these hurdles. I had no one to favour me so I proved my worth through my performances alone. Khoibi Sir acknowledged this later, once I started winning. He said that my ability was God-gifted. I functioned like a computer in the ring, he said, forward, backward, clockwise and anti-clockwise in complete command of the space.

Meanwhile, back home, Apa had to work twice as hard in my absence. Anu continued to do all she could to earn some extra money. I hardly went home. There were times when we did not meet for months. I went home only when I needed money or rice. Imphal was unfamiliar terrain for my parents, so they too did not venture there often. Apa farmed, Anu grew vegetables and wove clothes. They barely had time to enquire after my well-being. This did not upset me at all. I knew it was because their life was hard and not a lack of love or concern for me. Besides, it left me free to pursue excellence in boxing. As far as possible, I tried not to make any further demands on my parents, managing on whatever they could spare for me – Rs 50, occasionally Rs 100, a month.

I handled the many decisions and upheavals of life in Imphal – admission, choosing coaches, getting my gloves and guards – on my own. I bought my first gloves with Rs 350 that I had saved from my pocket money. In fact, at that point I hadn't even told my parents about my decision to take up boxing. I trained without proper equipment, because they were expensive. More than anything else, I wanted a pair of comfortable shoes, but I couldn't afford one. I managed with a pair bought from Moreh market, a cheap imitation of the original brands. Even when I went for the Nationals, my shoes were tattered – not that I let it bother me.

But I'm skipping ahead – before that came my first State Women's Boxing Championships. I was selected to play in the 48 kg category. But later, I was told that I'd have to play at a higher weight category to make way for another boxer. 'I'd rather not play at all,' I told the selection committee. I had just entered the world of boxing, and didn't want to start out by being manipulated. Eventually, they changed their mind. I went on to win the gold, and was also unanimously awarded the Best Boxer of the Tournament. Although there was no money to be won in this tournament, it secured me a place in the state selections and gave me a chance to prove myself at the national level. I was elated, but kept the joy to myself because my family didn't yet know about my shift to boxing. I had to find a way to let my parents know.

As it happened, the matter was taken out of my hands. A local newspaper reported on the State Championships with my name misspelt as 'Maki Kom'. Apa was on his way to Moirang on a cycle when he overheard a few men reading the local newspaper and talking about how even women had started boxing. He had cycled on quite a distance before he suddenly became curious about it. He went back to them and asked to see the paper. He read it through and peered at the grainy photograph. He didn't know of any Kom girl at SAI other than his own daughter.

But of course, his daughter was called 'Chungneijang', not 'Maki'. The thing is, when I first joined SAI Takyel, my friends couldn't get their tongues around my name. Coach Gosana pronounced it perfectly but almost no one else could. My friends told me that I should have a second name, one that could be easily pronounced. I kept thinking about it and then one day, on the spur of the moment, I told them to call me 'Mary'. The name would do both, signify my Christian faith and be easy to pronounce and remember. I informed my coach about my decision to change my name, but not my parents or relatives. In fact, one day Chungthang visited the Academy and asked for 'Chungneijang', but no one in the hostel knew anyone by that name. Finally he explained that he was looking for a 'Kom girl' and found out that I was now known as Mary. He was taken aback. When he met me that day, he advised me to also keep my original name, because it was derived from my grandmother's name and it would hurt her to see me lose it. That struck a chord. My name in official documents today is: Mangte Chungneijang Mary Kom, although I am mostly just called M.C. Mary Kom. 'Mary' has been a very lucky name for me.

To return to the story: Apa was still puzzled. He took the newspaper to Thangneireng Serto, one of the most educated men in my village. Serto explained that women's boxing was being developed as an independent sport, and that the newspaper reported that a 'Maki Kom' had won the gold. Uneasy, Father despatched my mother the next morning, telling her to bring me back on the pretext of discussing an urgent matter. Anu had to cajole me into returning home. I wasn't looking forward to confronting Apa.

The first thing he asked me was, 'Why? But why are you interested in boxing? You didn't even tell me about it. I had to learn about it from the newspaper'. With a stern look he added, 'I do not like it at all. Stop it before it's too late.'

'I like boxing, and will not stop. Please understand, Apa,' I said.

He paused to think about it and replied gently, 'You are a girl. One day, you will get married. Should anything happen, should you get injured, it will be a big problem. Many boxers get serious injuries; I have seen blood streaming down their faces. If you get injured, it will cost a lot of money, which I do not have.' Apa remembered that I used to devour martial arts movies, that I wanted to be like the fighters in them. 'If you're really interested in combat, why don't you join judo or karate?'

But I was adamant. I told him that boxing was my dream sport; I could not possibly give it up. I explained that amateur boxing was not as dangerous as he thought it was. I explained all the rules and about the protective gear we had to wear while playing.

Eventually he calmed down. He realized that I would not relent. He said that if I refused to give it up now, I must pursue it seriously, keep at it. Then he said that he felt incompetent as a father because I would be undernourished when compared to the others because of our financial problems. I assured him that I could manage without putting any additional burden on him. Of course, I had no idea how I might do this, or where I could find the stipends and funds I so badly needed. Everything looked bleak, but all I knew was that boxing was the only thing I really wanted to learn and master.

Now that Apa and my family knew, I felt a heavy load lift from my heart. This also meant that I was no longer struggling alone. Having made the decision to support me, my parents worked even harder. Anu began to weave even at night, with only the light of the boton to help her see. She used a traditional loin loom, every line woven into the fabric with both hands. She tried to finish a cloth in two days, more worried about quantity than quality. Apa would often help her stitch the cloth to get it ready in time for the next day. Years of working in the dim light have taken a toll on Anu's eyes, but without her support I couldn't have managed. She put aside every spare paisa and sent it to me so I could buy sporting kits and shoes.

The first time I went to meet Oja Ibomcha, he had commented on the gold earrings I wore. Those too had been bought with my mother's hard-earned extra income and they sat quite badly on my boyish face. I had desperately wanted shoes, like my friends in the village had, but Anu had insisted on buying me the gold. But that was then. Once my parents accepted that I was going to be a boxer, our resources were all redirected to support my dream.

There was this one time during those days in Imphal when I lost the money that Anu had sent me for a tracksuit. It was a princely sum and I didn't know how to tell her about it. Ultimately, I gathered the courage to do so. She didn't complain or grumble, just quietly went back to saving up enough all over again.

What did I hope to gain from my game and from putting my parents through all this? The truth is that I loved to play. My body was fit and my mind raring to go. But I also hoped that I would get a government job through the sports quota. I remember telling Anu: 'I will buy you lots of things one day. I will buy myself a Pulsar bike with my first prize money. For Apa, I'll buy a farm, and for you a four-wheeler.' It was a joke at the time, but also a secret wish. My father was cutting wood some distance away. He heard us and turned around to ask why we were laughing. Anu and I just laughed some more and cooked up even more elaborate dreams. My mom and dad are like friends to me, and moments like these only deepened my longing to help them live a better life.

The first time I stepped out of Manipur was for the Seventh East India Open Boxing Championships in Bengal. It was held at the South Kolkata Physical Culture Association in December 2000. Women's boxing wasn't a popular or recognized sport yet, so I was surprised when representatives of the Kom-Rem Student Union came to see me off at the bus station and presented me with Rs 500 and a traditional phanek – a sarong that Manipuri women wear – to encourage me and wish me well. They told me to wear the phanek on the victory stand. I felt then that I must win, not only for myself, but also my people.

Having lived my entire life in a village and a little of it in Imphal, I had no idea what the world outside was like. When I reached Guwahati and then crossed further beyond the Northeast, the first thing that struck me was that I had never seen so many people in one place. I was delighted by the pace and colour of this new world. I won a gold in that tournament, sealing a berth in the Manipur state team.

My first major tournament was the year after: the First National Women's Boxing Championships held in Chennai in 2001. I was chosen in the 48 kg category. Those days, I was young and had a pretty good appetite. It was a struggle to maintain that category. But I won a gold there too. The Manipur women's boxing team and Oja Kishan, who accompanied us, proceeded to Bangalore from there. That was my very first training camp.

At the camp, we followed a routine of different exercises for the various days of the week. There was speed training and workouts in the gym. I worked out on the pad to hit and perfect different punches, and used a punching bag to develop punching techniques. Shadow boxing, sparring bouts with different partners and various other forms of exercises were all part of the carefully planned regimen.

But the trip to Chennai was historic for me in one other way: it was the first time I travelled by train. I had expected the train to be bigger and cleaner, like in the movies. That was a disappointment. Besides, we were travelling without reservations, so we had to sit near the toilets. It was only later that I discovered that trains do have first-class and air-conditioned compartments. But back then, we had no money, so all of us travelled by the cheapest option. At least we were all together and that was fun.

I had often heard that Bangalore was one of the best cities in India. So when I found out that the training camp was to be there, I was very excited. But it didn't get off to a good start. I had just taken my luggage up to my room when a teammate arrived to tell me that our coach had summoned us. Leaving my things where they were, I went to the meeting, where Oja Kishan briefed us about the rules and regulations of the place. When I returned, my purse was gone, with all my money in it. So was the athlete I had seen in the room earlier. I had no idea that such things could happen. I knew no one in Bangalore and didn't know whom to ask for money. Finally, I called an uncle, Songboi Serto, in Imphal. He was a childhood friend of my father's and I had stayed with him for a few months in Imphal. His friend in Mangalore, Angam Rimai, travelled forty kilometres to bring me some money. To this day I remember that incident with relief and gratitude. I also wonder at the network of the tiny Kom community that it managed to provide help to a young girl stranded with no support so far away from home.

This was no isolated incident either. Over and over again in my sporting journey, family, friends and strangers have helped and supported me. There were, for instance, Uncle L. Lenpu and his wife Kipnu in Imphal, who had asked my father if they could adopt me and take care of my needs. Uncle had a strong intuition that I could be successful if I had the right support and guidance.

Another overwhelming memory is of my journey to Hisar for training and selection to the First Asian Women's Boxing Championship Meet, also in 2001. We had planned this journey in advance and our tickets were booked. Then we were told that the Manipur Boxing Association was organizing the Churachand Memorial Boxing Tournament and that it was compulsory for all national-level players to compete. This was shattering news because the Hisar training camp was also a selection camp for an international championship. Rajesh Bhandari of the Indian Amateur Boxing Federation (IABF) questioned why the Manipur team was missing from Hisar. He called the secretary of MABA and told him that our presence in the camp was compulsory. So once again, we prepared to go to Hisar. We managed to get tickets, but not in the same compartment. This time I was extra careful and locked my suitcase to the seat with an iron chain. We were passing through Bihar at night. When I woke up, as the train pulled into Gorakhpur, I saw that the chain had been cut and my suitcase stolen. This time it wasn't only money but all my belongings – including my passport, which I had obtained in advance, hoping to be selected for the international competition – that had been stolen. I burst into loud sobs. It was more than I could deal with. I even considered jumping off the train and just dying. But I couldn't do that to my parents. My friends and our coach tried to console me, and assured me that they would all do what they could to help. We reached Delhi, reported the loss at a police station and then proceeded to Hisar.

Although my coach and friends contributed money for my immediate needs, I was so anguished that I called Apa and told him that I wanted to die. 'Don't say things like that. I will do all I can to get you a new passport. You concentrate on your training,' he assured me. But how would they raise that sort of money again? I couldn't concentrate. Later, I learnt that they had sold our only cow, my brother's favourite pet. Apparently, he had cried for long after her new owners took the cow away. My mother set herself to working almost without a break to raise the money. But, of course, none of this would be quite enough.

My parents are proud people who would not stoop to borrowing as long as they could earn with their own hands, even if it meant working through the day and night. As my needs and expenses increased, they stretched themselves through blood and sweat to meet my demands.

At Hisar I was selected for the championship. But without a passport I would be replaced. Although he was reluctant to trouble anyone or ask for favours, my father visited Uncle Songboi, who came to my rescue once again. He reproached my father for not telling him earlier and entrusted a certain L. Songkhup Kom with the responsibility of collecting money from among the Koms in the Greater Imphal area. He also telephoned an officer in the passport office whom he was acquainted with. The officer told him, 'A new passport in a day? Mr Songboi, you are asking for a miracle.' But when the situation was explained to him, he did indeed perform that little bit of magic. Uncle Songboi's brother, Ahmang, flew to Guwahati with all the required documents. Another uncle, L. Kailun, who was the superintendent of police, Imphal East, helped speed up the paperwork. As soon as the passport was ready, it was despatched to Delhi, where Onler Kom – whom I knew, if not very well back then – collected it and set off to deliver it to me in Hisar, six hours away. It was a turning point in our friendship.

It was a surreal moment when I held the passport in my hand. I heaved a massive sigh of relief and sent up a prayer for the goodwill of friends and relatives, and the tireless efforts of my parents.

I had been praying earnestly all this while, of course, trying to find a way to calm my anxiety. In the course of those prayers I had thought about the talisman father had given me. His friends had given it to him and told him that it would ward off evil and protect me. I had tied it around my arm to please him. It occurred to me now that believing in charms was contradictory to our faith, so I took it off and threw it away. I decided instead to believe in God. It may sound strange to you, my readers, especially those of you who have never been believers, but ever since I threw that talisman away, my run of bad luck ended.

I was able to travel to Bangkok – another first, my first foreign journey. But all the stress and worry took its toll and I was defeated in my very first bout. My confidence was at its lowest then. When I saw my opponent – bigger than me, with well-formed muscles – I became nervous. She looked strong and confident and had the support of the home crowd. I went down tamely.

But it was a big lesson for me. I vowed that I would never give up so easily again, that I would fight with my mind as well as with my body. The next international meet was only a few months away: the World Championships in the US. I would make my mark there, I promised myself.

4

My first international medal

Soon after the Bangkok championship, I was selected in the 48-kg category for the International Boxing Association (originally the Association Internationale de Boxe Amateur, or the AIBA) World Women's Boxing Championships in Pennsylvania, USA, in November–December 2001.

My father managed to collect only Rs 2,000 for my trip. I was both upset and very worried because I'd heard of how expensive things were in America. But there was nothing my parents or I could do. I spoke to Onler about my problem. He invited a few students and elders from our community and organized a meeting to discuss ways to raise money for the trip. Pu. Lalkhomang, president of the Kom-Rem Union, Manipur, was visiting Delhi then and was present at the meeting. He suggested that the students should meet the two members of Parliament (MPs) from Manipur and seek their help. They did just that. The two MPs – Holkhomang Haokip and Choaba Singh – donated Rs 5,000 and Rs 3,000 respectively and I suddenly had Rs 10,000 in my hands. With this princely sum, and a little more that had been collected from the community, I left for the US. I was relieved to have money in my pocket, and knew that I could not come back empty-handed after all the efforts that people had made on my behalf.

Pennsylvania was cold and beautiful. It was snowing. We were confined to the sports arena, but what little I saw was pleasing to the eye. The people there were enormously nice too. It was the first time in my life that I had travelled so far. I was looking forward to seeing what America was all about. But since we were the last team to arrive, we went straight to the sporting arena from the airport. The other teams had already completed their weighing in, which is compulsory for all players. I was very tired and suffering from jet lag. It had been morning when I left, and here it was morning again. After the weighing in, I found out that I did not have any match that day. I was fortunate, but some of my team-mates were not so lucky. I was able to rest well enough to face my opponent in the first round, which I won comfortably. My fear of facing new opponents quickly vanished. I competed in the 48 kg in this championship. While my team-mates lost one after the other, I went on to reach the finals. I was even hopeful of winning the gold. The boxers were not unbeatable as I had earlier thought.

I felt like this would be the place, the event, that would change my life. I felt more confident. I kept telling myself, 'I can face anyone in the ring.' In the quarter-final, I defeated Nadia Hokmi of Poland by RSC (Referee Stopped Contest – applicable if the referee feels one of the boxers is inferior to the other and risks getting hurt badly), and in the semi-final, I defeated Jamie Behl of Canada 21–9. I reached the finals, but lost to Hula Sahin of Turkey 13–5.

The greatest disadvantage for me was my loss of appetite. I was not accustomed to the food there. Try as I might, I could not eat the food and I started to lose weight. So much so that just before the finals I was only 46 kg. This is probably what cost me my dream of winning gold and I was very disappointed. I went to my room and cried. I was convinced that I was being punished because I had fought with my father just before I left for the US. But the coaches were kind; they consoled me and lauded me on the silver win. I was the only one in the team to get a medal. But the biggest thing I took away from this championship was the conviction that I could take on any boxer.

Everything in the US was awfully expensive. I returned home with a few candies for my family, and the Rs 2,000 that Apa had given me.

In the course of my career, I have become used to travel and to the different ways that things work in other countries. But I remember this trip to the US with complete clarity. During practice, I would sweat profusely, so right after play, I needed a hot bath to prevent my body from becoming stiff. The bathroom had a bathtub, which I wasn't used to. It had two taps, one with 'H' written in red, and the other with 'C' written in blue. The first time, I opened the 'H' tap and left the room. When I went back to check, the water was only lukewarm. Too embarrassed to ask someone what the problem might be, I quietly bathed in that barely warm water in the cold winter.

That wasn't the only time. The plumbing in many European countries is so different from what we have at home. Once I turned a tap the wrong way and hot water came gushing out, scalding my hands. And the electric switches are also so unfamiliar that it takes me a while to figure out the right way to get a light or the air conditioner working. At times I've slept with the light on the whole night because I couldn't manage to switch it off and was too embarrassed to ask for help.

My friends must have had their own share of embarrassing experiences but most of us were too shy to relate these even to each other. I did share some of my stories with Sarita and Jenny, and we all laughed about them together.

Another time, in China, we were given chopsticks to eat our meals with. Just when I had painfully begun to master the art of using a knife and fork, I had to use two sticks to fill my stomach. I ended up using both my hands to hold the chopstick to pick up the food and push it into my mouth. My teammates asked for spoons but I tried to manage with the sticks. It helped that I really enjoy Chinese food. I was hungry enough that I managed the complex work required – I ate enough to sate my appetite and my palate. In fact, as far as food is concerned, I like most of the food in Asia, but Continental food is too sweet for my liking. After five years of travelling, I started taking along some packed food from home, including chutney, dried meat and fish to get me through my stays in European countries.

Back home the media was not even remotely interested in the fact that an Indian had won the silver in the first edition of a world championship event. Women's boxing was at a nascent stage and was yet to attract fans or critics.

On my return, however, the Kom-Rem Students' Union and other members of my community in Delhi gave me a warm welcome at the airport. Back in Imphal, I was greeted with garlands and drumbeats and dancing. There was a victory ride across town and a felicitation programme was held in Langol, an area that houses the government quarters. Thanksgiving prayers were said and words of praise and adulation were showered on me. I was presented with a traditional shawl. Oja Ibomcha was also present and was duly felicitated. The day ended with a grand feast.

My community was proud that I was now an international-level boxer. It was the first sporting achievement of its kind by anyone in our small tribe. To be honest, one of the greatest motivating forces for me has been my desire to assert the identity of my tribe 'Kom' within my own country and the world over. We are just a few thousand people. I hoped that by coming up in sports and getting known worldwide, I'd be able to popularize the culture and ethos of my tiny tribe. When I spoke to the people in Langol that day, I spoke about these things and of my hope that I would win gold in future tournaments.

Anu had borrowed money from her sister to hire a vehicle to bring my family to Imphal, so excited was she at my achievement. We had been through a lot as a family so I could get where I had and it looked like, finally, things would change for us; that all our sacrifices were worth it. It seemed like my decision to leave my family and go away to Imphal despite our meagre resources had been the right one.

The medal certainly helped our finances in a big way. The Sports Ministry announced a cash award of Rs 9 lakh. It's another matter that it took almost a year before Uma Bharati, the sports minister at the time, finally handed the cheque to me at a function in Delhi.

The first thing I did with the prize money was to buy a paddy field for Apa. He would no longer be a landless farmer in an agricultural society. Our family celebrated with a Thanksgiving feast. I then set aside money for the education of my brother and sister. They had been denied a lot to make my dream possible and it was only fair that I repay them. The cheque might have been for me, in acknowledgement of my achievements, but my boxing career wasn't just about me, it was about my whole family. We were in it together in every way.

And where would I be without the Manipur boxing establishment? I expressed my gratitude to them when I donated a small sum of money to the MABA. I conveyed my thanks to my coaches, Oja Ibomcha, Oja Narjit, Oja Kishan and Oja Khoibi Salam (secretary of the MABA) because it was their effort to make Manipuri women world-class boxers that helped me translate my ambition into success.

Oh, and I did buy myself a two-wheeler, although Anu dissuaded me from buying a Pulsar. I settled for the more feminine Activa. Women in Manipur drive two-wheelers because it is the easiest way to commute from one place to another. It gives us independence and saves time.

The rest of the money I set aside for my training and travels. I had to be thrifty and spend only on the most urgent needs. My career had only just begun. While my parents no longer needed to spend sleepless nights thinking about providing for me, or themselves, even the remarkable sum of Rs 9 lakh could not fund every dream I had. I needed more.

That first international medal, a silver, will always mean a lot to me. The fight and all that followed are clearly etched in my memory. But deep inside, I was not happy with a silver. As I touched down in India, I vowed that the next time I would bring back a gold. I knew I was good enough.

5

Onler and I

I had been away from home for two years by now. As supportive as my parents had been, they were simple folk. I often wished for someone I could turn to for support and guidance when things got complicated or lonely – personally as well as professionally. I was spending more and more time away from home. Very often, I couldn't return even for Christmas. It was a sacrifice I was willing to make, but it did get lonely. My only friends were from the world of boxing.

I had given up my studies for the sport. The only languages I knew were Manipuri and my own Kom language. Outside Manipur, I became acutely conscious of my inability to communicate effectively in either Hindi or English.

It was at such a time that I met Onler Kom, and though I didn't know it then, it was a meeting that would change my life completely. I was in Delhi during a training session in 2000 when Onler and a friend of his came to see me. He was then the president of the Kom-Rem Students' Union in Delhi and was pursuing a degree in Law. He was responsible for the welfare of Kom students in Delhi, one of the most popular destinations for students from the Northeast. Onler had been entrusted with the responsibility of looking me up and briefing me about the union and its activities.

I was quite surprised to hear that I had a visitor because I didn't know anybody in Delhi. We shook hands and spoke a little. He was much older than me and I thought of him almost as a concerned, older brother. Before he left he told me that I must get in touch with him if I needed any help.

When there was a break in the camp I called Onler to let him know that I was going home. I asked him if he wanted anything from Manipur. He was surprised that I had called, and with an offer, not a request. I had brought back some home-made food and dry fish, and offered to drop some off at the house he had rented in Munirka. At the time, I was only repaying his gesture of friendship to me in a strange city where I knew no one.

What really deepened our friendship was his concern over my lost passport when I was in Hisar. He followed up on progress back in Manipur and as soon as the passport reached Delhi, set off to deliver it to me. I came to regard him truly as an older brother and guardian then.

I began confiding in him and sharing my worries, and explained to him how my parents struggled to send me Rs 1,000 every month. I told him how they would sometimes neglect my siblings' school fees to send me the money I needed. My brother and sister had to face the humiliation of standing outside their classrooms and not being able to appear for their exams.

Onler advised me to be frugal and suggested ways in which I could save money. Being a sports lover himself, Onler understood the depth of my passion for boxing and encouraged me to do my best. I looked forward to meeting him now and then. I also met his friends Benhur, Ahao and Paul, his cousin Boite and several others every time I visited Delhi for training camps or on the way to tournaments elsewhere. In the company of Onler and his friends, I felt less homesick.

Onler's support before I left for Pennsylvania in 2001 only served to deepen our friendship. When I returned with the silver, we grew closer. I knew that his concern for my well-being was sincere. I liked the attention he showered on me and often sought his advice. He was my emotional anchor.

My life had become an unending series of tours and training sessions. I had little time to socialize. On Sundays, when I had a little free time, Onler and I would meet, and we'd eat a home-cooked meal with friends and relatives. It was very de-stressing for me. We shared a language and background, which helped me relax in Onler's company. He followed my career closely and wanted to help me reach as far as I could. He only had sage advice and cautionary words for me.

Onler was nursing a broken heart those days after the end of a long-term relationship and he told me as much frankly. His mother had passed away recently, and Onler often felt like going back home to be with his family. But his father had urged him to pursue higher studies, so he had enrolled in the LLB course.

Meanwhile, women's boxing was becoming a popular sport. In 2003, I received the Arjuna Award, which was a huge boost for my career. With this, my ratings in the marriage market shot up too. Back home, young and old suitors began to approach my parents. In my work sphere too, I began to get a lot of unwanted attention from admirers. All of this made me restless and uncomfortable. I spoke to Onler about the situation.

'Mary, why are you getting all these proposals? Are you interested in marriage?' he asked me.

I was stuck for an answer. Marriage was not on my agenda; all I wanted to do was to play and win. I also wanted with all my heart to participate in the Olympics, whenever women's boxing became a recognized sport.

Onler was worried that I would give up my career once I got married, as was common among women sportspersons. I was startled that he should say such a thing. I thought he, of all people, understood that the 'gold medal haul' (as people were calling it those days) was not easy at all. I had put everything else in my life aside to spend five or six hours every day working out and keeping fit. I practised my techniques with single-minded devotion, fought bouts in the ring with different sparring partners, threw punches at bags to perfect my jabs. Then there was the fact that I was constantly travelling, getting ready for one championship or the other. The level of competition rose with every tournament. I couldn't afford to be caught off-guard even for the National Championships. Where was the time for romance?

I did not realize that Onler was being updated with news from home. He was upset by the fact that so many proposals were coming in for me. I began to sense a change in his attitude. He was worried that my parents would accept a proposal without my consent and force me into a marriage. His imagination went wild. He even believed that someone might use black magic to charm me. That particular fear was rooted in the fact that Koms were believed to be experts in black magic. Before the advent of Christianity, using charms and magic was the way of life among our tribe. While we do brush aside these stories as just folklore, traces of the old culture linger. Onler felt compelled by his need to protect me.

A wrong partner would definitely be the end of my career. Since I was young and quite naïve, he feared that I would be swayed by the attentions of these suitors. It wasn't unheard of for sportspeople to have romantic affairs.

I was touched by his concern. We had been close for a few years and he understood my temperament, my whims and fears, my passion for boxing, my need to defend my title. Simply put, he felt he knew me best.

What I didn't realize was that Onler's feelings for me had gone through a sudden transformation, almost like the switching on of a light bulb. He wanted to be more than a friend or an older brother. Having made up his mind to reveal his feelings for me, he invited Jenny and me to lunch on Sunday. Jenny is a boxer from Mizoram and a good friend of mine. We were together in most camps. Like any other lunch get-together at his place, we cooked our favourite dishes. After a great meal, we chatted and joked until it was time for Jenny and me to leave. When I returned to the hostel, Onler called, which was highly unusual. I wondered if I'd left something behind.

'Hello?'

'Have you reached the hostel safely?' he asked.

'Yes? Did you have something to say?'

Long pause. 'May I say something?'

'Yes, of course, Onler. Do say what you need to.'

Long pause again.

I was beginning to get impatient. 'Say it. What is it? I am all ready to listen.' Maybe he wants to make a declaration of love, I thought to myself, smiling. But I was also beginning to get tired of holding a silent phone.

Then, mustering all his courage, Onler said, 'I think you should understand what I'm trying to say even if I don't speak the words out loud.'

With that he put the phone down. I was very surprised. When Onler was quiet and hesitant, I knew what he wanted to say. I expected him to say the magic words – 'I love you' – or at least something to that effect but they never came. I would later joke with Onler that he proposed to me on the phone, that too without actually saying anything.

But this sudden change in him threw me. Now that I was conscious of his feelings for me, I was embarrassed about meeting him. I avoided him for a long time. Finally, he rang up Jenny to enquire about me and invited us both for lunch. Blissfully ignorant of the tension between Onler and me, Jenny accepted. I was reluctant to go but she was so insistent that I had to tag along eventually. I was nervous because I'd be seeing Onler after a long time. I felt my heart beating loudly like a drum and wondered whether people could actually hear it. I was mostly quiet through lunch. I no longer felt as free as I did before. Once we were done with lunch Jenny and I prepared to leave. Onler whispered to me, 'Please think about my proposal.'

It certainly did keep me thinking. I played out various scenarios in my head, like I did with my boxing bouts – the moves, hits, punches, perfect deliveries. I did not doubt Onler's affection and care. He helped me in every way he could. He understood and supported my passion for sports. He knew about my humble background and did not put me down for it. Onler understood the world around us better than I did. We were from the same community. What more do I need, I asked myself.

Then one day he visited me alone and took me out for a 'talk'. Over a cup of tea, he explained why he had proposed to me. 'I want to protect your career, and that is one of the main reasons for my proposal,' he declared. I didn't say anything, and he took that for a yes. 'I want to meet your parents. Will they accept me? If I go and ask for your hand in marriage, will they agree? If I offer to boil tea for them, will your father drink it in acceptance of the proposal?' He said it all so rapidly that it took me a while to understand the full import of what he was saying. He was proposing marriage.

For a while I was stumped. Then my mind was racing. A friendship and a relationship I could handle, but I didn't think I was ready for marriage, or to make a lifelong commitment. I was in my early twenties. My career looked promising. I had a busy schedule of tours and training. It was hard for me to think beyond boxing. How would marriage fit into my life?

On the other hand, in Onler I had found a soulmate who understood my ambition. I did need someone by my side to help me and anchor me emotionally. Someone like him. As I thought about it, my feelings took a complete U-turn. It just happened.

Onler had not taken the trouble to woo me with roses. There were no romantic dinners, long walks and chit-chats. He was a straightforward person who laid out the facts, like a boxer delivering punches to the face. Perhaps that's what won me over. His actions spoke louder than his words. I had to give him an answer. Then I had to tell my parents.

If Onler's proposal was unromantic, my response was just as prosaic. 'Will you let me continue playing?'

He took my hand and, holding it, looked into my eyes as he made the promise. 'I will never come between you and your career.'

Onler called his father to share the news with him. He asked if his dad knew 'Mary Kom, the woman boxer from Kangathei.' Onler's father said he knew my grandparents, and that Onler's mother was closely related to my grandfather.

We realized then that we shared common roots and fate had brought us together.

Onler's father was against the idea of our relationship. And persuading my parents, I knew, would be another matter altogether. I had known Onler since 2001, but my parents had never met him. Our courtship was conducted in Delhi.

Knowing my father's temper, I was scared to break the news to him. My career was beginning to look up and my financial situation had improved. My parents were bound to think that marriage would be the end of my ambition. So, even though Onler kept pressuring me to meet my parents, I kept putting it off.

Sure enough, when I finally mustered the courage to tell them, Apa told me stop seeing Onler and concentrate on my sport without the bother and hindrance of a marriage. I pleaded with him to meet Onler before he passed judgement on him.

So far, as the many proposals kept pouring in, Apa had resolutely turned them down. He wanted me to focus on my boxing and to improve my ratings. Naturally, he wasn't happy with Onler's proposal either.

Finally, in 2004, Onler and I decided to go to Manipur and face the music. He wanted to meet my parents first, before his father went to meet them. What if they refuse, I asked him. He paid no heed and prepared to meet them by himself. I informed my parents that he would be visiting.

He took a bus from his village to Moirang and walked two-and-a-half kilometres to my house in Kangathei. He describes it as a long, hot journey. Anu received him at the gate and brought him in. But Apa's countenance changed to a 'deathly look' (as Onler puts it) upon seeing him.

'Who are you?' Apa asked.

'I am Onler, son of Rekhupthang Karong, chief of Samulamlan village.'

'You ...,' my father paused to control his rage, 'are you thinking of putting an end to my daughter's career? Why are you disturbing her? Are you showing me disrespect?' My father was not pleased with Onler's visit and did not bother with playing the gracious host. Without even looking at his visitor's face, he continued, 'Don't follow my daughter around. If you don't help her, there will be others who will. I don't want you acting smart, trying to convince me.'

I felt sorry for Onler, because my father did not give him a chance to speak. Finally, patiently, he explained that he truly loved and cared for me. He wanted to marry me and take care of me, even if it meant putting his own career on the line. He had even given up his job in Customs and Excise to be near me.

Apa was not convinced by all this. As Onler stood up to leave, my father coldly told him not to send his family over for any negotiations. Anu was very upset with Apa's behaviour, and so was I. But I knew better than to expect anything else of him. Anu and I walked a short distance with Onler, who pleaded with her once again to understand his true intentions. He wanted to be by my side, especially because I was often travelling by bus or train and it could be unsafe for a young girl. 'What if someone forcibly abducts her and marries her?' he asked. Anu was supportive and asked him to send his family to our house for a 'talk'. She promised that she would do her best to convince Apa. Her kind words lifted his spirits as he made his way back to his own village.

The traditional manner in which a boy's family asks for a girl's hand in marriage is by boiling tea in the girl's house. This is done thrice before the date of the wedding is finalized. The first time Onler's father came, my maternal uncle welcomed him warmly. The first boiling-tea session is usually a hush-hush affair, to be done only by two or three members of the boy's family – usually only the parents. If the girl's parents accept the proposal, they drink the tea. When Onler's father came to my house with a few family members, Apa did not even allow them to enter the house.

Apa's childish behaviour embarrassed and angered me. I left home and went to a friend's place. My parents searched all over, but couldn't find me. They became frantic. Anu even called Onler to enquire. He was so worried that he borrowed a scooter and rushed to Moirang. Unable to enter my house, he sent someone to ask if I had returned. By then, I had. He then went back to Imphal, where his sister lives.

Early next morning, I packed a few of my things and went to Imphal. I intended to elope with Onler. I was still angry and felt let down by my father.

'Let's get married, with or without my parents' approval. And then let's go to Delhi,' I told Onler.

He calmed me down, and said, 'Mary, you are the eldest. You should not act like this. I am also the last one in my family to get married. We should not disgrace our families.'

By then, my mother had come to take me back home. Anu knew that Onler was in Imphal, so his was the first house she went to. Onler assured and reassured me that he would talk to my father again, and with that to strengthen me I reluctantly followed Anu home. Another day, I made a second attempt to convince Onler to leave home, but he firmly refused.

Our family had endured many hardships together so I could follow my passion, and now Apa couldn't understand why I was willing to lose everything just when things were finally looking up. But slowly he cooled down and began to see the honour in Onler's intentions, and also that he did not take advantage of my vulnerability. Knowing my temperament, Apa knew I was unlikely to back down.

When I had calmed down somewhat, I had a heart-to-heart chat with him. 'You cannot help me. Don't you know how difficult it is to get things done without help?'

Apa relented and sent a messenger to Onler's family to come and boil tea at our house.

Putting the previous episode behind them, Onler's family came and boiled tea again in February 2004. This time, my parents drank gladly. The second time tea was boiled, his father came with prominent elders of the family. The most important is the third tea-boiling ceremony when there is a big gathering of relatives and friends from both families. Onler's family brought sweets and delicacies to the event. This was a public declaration of our engagement. After the ceremony, which was held in November 2004, the elders fixed a date for our marriage. With that, I was officially betrothed to Onler.

Our community has a custom that requires the groom's family to pay the bride a price that the woman's family demands. People expected that my father would quote a high price but all he asked for was the traditional cloth meant for the parents of the bride. Usually, parents of the bride demand a pair of bullocks or some money. But my father insisted that all he wanted was for the two families to come together in warmth and understanding, and wish for the love and happiness of the two children.

The wedding date was set for 12 March 2005. It was to be my last Christmas with my parents and siblings. My parents no longer needed to work so hard but being accustomed to labour and toil, they kept busy with the farm, kitchen garden and household chores.

My youngest sister was only two years old then. There is an amusing story about the birth of my sister. Anu was working so hard to provide for my needs that she did not even realize that, after a gap of sixteen years, she had conceived again. I was busy those days and seldom went home. I am not sure why my parents did not inform me about the pregnancy. When I returned home, I saw Anu with a baby. 'Am I dreaming?' I asked my father. Getting over my shock, I went up to my mother and the baby. The moment I held the frail girl in my arms, I fell in love with her. I decided to name her 'Cindy'. She brought luck to the family. Soon after she was born, I started winning national and international championships. I became very attached to my youngest sister and would have her stay with me even after marriage. It's only after my twins came along that she stopped staying with me.

My sister and brother were in high school by now, and old enough to understand that I would soon be leaving. We spent a beautiful Christmas together – singing, dancing and feasting with friends and relatives in the village. At home, we sat by the fire, talking, joking, reminiscing and feeling grateful for God's blessings.

After the festivities were over, preparations for the wedding began in earnest. I had no idea how to select a wedding dress, because the only fashion I knew was sportswear, track suits and the like. Our friends said that wedding gowns were much more reasonably priced in Delhi than in Imphal, so we shopped for one there. I settled on a gown that cost Rs 20,000 for the whole set, along with the flowers and hand bouquet. I was being extravagant, but I wanted the day to be special.

According to our custom, the wedding ceremony is held in the boy's house. The modern trend in Manipur is that a day or two before the wedding, there is a send-off party, or a bridal shower, for the bride-to-be. I had mine on 11 March in Kangathei. I was supposed to give a farewell speech as part of the programme. I dreaded that moment and had to work hard to compose myself. As I started on my speech, I realized how painful it was to leave behind everything that had been a part of me for so long – the good times and the hard times. I thanked my family for their love and all the sacrifices they made for me. Then all the elders spoke, bidding me to be a dutiful wife and a good daughter-in-law, and bestowing their blessings on me. As the wedding choir sang a farewell song, I cried freely once again. We ended the day with a feast.

My parents had arranged for a few necessary items, like a bed, pots and pans and traditional shawls (called saipikhup, ponchai and ponkokhui) to be presented to the groom's family. I had to take shawls and sarongs for everyone in my new family, particularly the elders. On his part, Onler was supposed to bring similar gifts for my family. This was meant to signify the growing harmony between the two houses.

12 March 2005 dawned fresh and warm, a beautiful spring day. The wedding would take place at the Manipur Baptist Convention Church, one of the biggest churches in Imphal. Walking down the aisle with my father, I was nervous about being watched so closely. I was more comfortable being watched in a boxing ring. But at the end of it, Onler was waiting for me, to hold my hands and say 'I do'. We pledged to 'love, honour, cherish, to have and to hold in sickness and in health, for richer or for poorer, for as long as we both live', and exchanged rings to seal our vows. It remains one of the most beautiful days of my life.

The wedding reception was held at Onler's village, sixty kilometres from Imphal. The festivity, feasting, singing and dancing continued late into the night.

I took a four-month break from boxing so I could ease into my new life. After the wedding we stayed at Samulamlan, my new village and home, for about a month. I learnt to adapt to my new family and got to know them. Before I left home, the elders in my family had told me to wake up early, do the household chores, cook and serve my in-laws. I had been worried about whether I would fit in and what they would expect of me. My fears were unfounded. Ours was a joint family, comprising the two of us, Onler's younger brother, Songneireng, his wife Lamneikim, and my father-in-law. My sister-in-law wouldn't let me do anything.

My father-in-law was particularly concerned about my comfort. He woke up very early and would call to my husband, 'On, get up. It's time to help me with some work.'

Onler would taunt me saying, 'You are a girl. You should be the one to get up.'

His father, on hearing us bickering, would say, 'On, let her sleep. She needs rest. You get up. She is home just for a few days, so let her sleep. Don't disturb her.'

I will never forget the love he showered on me. As it turned out, the short time we spent together was one of the last occasions that we would be together as a whole family.

A month later we returned to Imphal. By then the Government of Manipur had allotted me a house at the National Games Village. The Village had been built for the athletes participating in the 1999 National Games and was later turned into government quarters. The earlier occupants of A/112 had just vacated, so we had to wait until the house was cleaned and renovated. We stayed in a rented accommodation until we could begin our married life in our new house.

I was glad to be able to set up my home before I had to travel again on work. My mother is a simple woman, with no knowledge of the finer ways of life, but she had taught me how to run a home impeccably. I had even learnt the art of weaving from her.

Soon enough, it was time to go back to camp and begin training for the Asian Boxing Championships and World Championships. True to his word, Onler raised no objections. He dropped me off at the first camp. It was a great feeling to be travelling as husband and wife. I suffered separation pangs, of course, but in the years that followed, I left my husband to go from camp to camp.

Onler knew from the beginning that ours would be an unusual marriage. A wife who is absent for most of the year cannot run the home. In our society, the woman runs the house, even if she is a career woman. The kitchen is her domain; she is the one who shops for vegetables and groceries. In fact, the market is a place where women sell goods and other women buy them. Imphal's Ima Market – or Mother's Market – is fairly well known, even something of a tourist attraction. Women in salaried jobs have been known to augment their income by sitting in Ima Market in the evenings.

In our case, Onler runs the house and fulfils social obligations, like visiting ailing relatives or attending weddings and funerals. He tackled problems by himself, like when essential commodities – gas or baby formula –became unavailable. Onler had to cope with all this on his own.

The mobile phone is a crucial thread that keeps us going through our long-distance marriage. When I get lonely or miss home, he speaks loving, encouraging words to me. When I cry, he consoles me. When I need to talk, I know I can say what I want to, holding nothing back.

People often ask us about trust. I go globetrotting and spend my time with men, young and old. Does Onler never suspect my loyalty? I have only this to say: I grew up in a family where values were held in high esteem. Marriage is a sacred commitment. Onler knows that I would never do anything to blemish our marriage. If he felt otherwise, I have no doubt that he would have put an end to my globetrotting. People refer to Onler as 'Mary's husband', but I know that behind Mary's success, there is Onler.

He is the reason my medal hauls continued after the marriage, putting an end to doomsday predictions about the end of my career.

6

Back to work

The silver in Pennsylvania and the prize money from the government had put an end to my immediate financial worries. But I wanted a job too, for that alone can bring long-term security and a steady income. Also, around the time that I was getting married, I had no savings except a couple of life insurance policies. We had a lot of dependents and even my travel for work cost money. Players often end up spending out of their pocket for at least some of the travel-related expenses. That aside, the career of a sportsperson is a short one. I even went to Haryana to try my luck in the police recruitment there, but did not get selected. Back home, though, the first two World Championship medals landed me a job as a police constable. I declined it, because I didn't think it was an adequate reward for a player who had just brought home a World Championship silver and a gold. After my second World Championship gold, the Manipur government offered me the post of sub-inspector, which I accepted in 2005. I had long dreamt of getting a government job through the sports quota, and it was finally fulfilled. That year was twice blessed: I landed a job and a life partner in Onler.

I earned a salary of Rs 15,000 in that first job. The thing about jobs that are obtained through the sports quota is that we are not required to go in to work as regularly as our colleagues because we tend to be away at camps and tournaments through much of the year. I go to office when necessary. And every time I need to go out of station, I am required to take leave and inform the department.

My medal haul continued after my marriage, putting an end to speculation among my family and friends around that particular topic. I retained the world title in the Third World Women's Boxing Championships at Podolsk in Russia, in 2005. Sarita, who had won the bronze, and I were given a heroes' welcome at the Imphal airport. We were taken to the Bhagyachandra Open Air Theatre, where a grand reception was organized.

I'd had a good run from 2001 to 2004. I won several golds: all the Senior Women's National Championships; the 2nd World Women's Boxing Championships, 2002; the 2nd Asian Women's Boxing Championships at Hisar in 2003; and the Witch Cup Boxing Championships at Paes, Hungary. In spite of this, when I got married, my two families, friends, fans and even my own community were doubtful that my medal hauls would continue. But after the wedding, I participated in and won a gold in the Third and Fourth World Women's Boxing Championships in October 2005 and November 2006.

There were a number of other international-level championships, in Taiwan, Vietnam, Denmark and so on. But it was retaining my world title in 2006 by defeating Steluta Duta of Romania 22–7 at the Fourth World Championships in New Delhi that I consider one of my greatest achievements.

I had a cold and fever through the tournament, but for fear of doping charges, I did not take medication for it. It was my willpower that saw me through it all.

Curiously, the fact that the basic medicines one takes for a cold or cough somehow always show up as positive for banned substances, is something friends have told me – not coaches or doctors. Athletes are, more often than not, unaware of how doping really works. I believe it is the responsibility of our coaches to keep track of the banned substances and advice us on what medicines to take or avoid. I don't know if my friends were right about the cold and cough medicines, but the fear of testing positive kept me from taking a chance (or a medicine).

But to return to my Delhi win, it is probably the most memorable for me because I was able to win at home, in front of my husband, my father-in-law and my relatives, all of whom had come to watch the match. Later, we went sightseeing in and around Delhi with my father-in-law – a particularly precious memory because he passed away soon after. Apa did not come to Delhi that time, but Anu did. She accompanied us on the sightseeing tour.

The other Indian boxers also performed exceptionally well. India won four golds, one silver and three bronzes, and our team won the overall title.

With this hat-trick of World Championship wins, the media christened me 'Queen of Boxing' and 'Magnificent Mary'. Around this time, there were also proposals to name the approach to Langol Games Village 'Mary Kom Road', although there was no official declaration at the time. With all the celebrations and felicitations, I had barely any time to spend with my husband and in-laws. But Christmas 2006 was spent at home in Samulamlan. It was a beautiful, perfect day. We had no premonition of what was to happen only a few days later.

7

The other face of Manipur

My own life had been limited to coping with the hardships of poverty and then the rigours of my sporting life. But that one incident woke me up to the reality of the world around me.

Manipur has been an insurgency-torn state since the 1980s. With a population of a mere twenty-seven lakh, it is home to over thirty militant groups. They are best known to the outside world by their acronyms, most notably NSCN-IM, NSCN-K, UNLF and KNO.

These groups dominate different areas where they run parallel governments, each with its own constitution and vision for the future. People who live in remote villages with no police or army security are the most vulnerable. Chiefs of villages are given demand letters, and if they fail to fulfil the militants' wishes, they are kidnapped, very often never to return. Sometimes the demand is for supplies, at other times that the village should arrange recruits for one or the other organization.

Mary at the 6th AIBA Women's
World Boxing Championships 2010
in Barbados

Mid-fight, Mary is a
picture of concentration

All focus and concentration
in training, as in
competitions

Small and sinewy: at the
National Championships 2011
in Bhopal

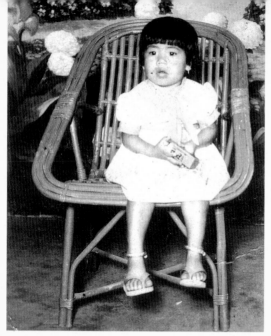

Mary Kom at four years of age

Mary was fiercely protective of her younger siblings as a child

Mary, aged fourteen, in the school uniform that made her parents so proud

Kneeling in church in their wedding finery

The exchange of wedding rings

Onler and Mary as man and wife

A marriage and a partnership that set Mary free to seek her dream

Mary is an ardent champion of children's rights

On a rare and well-deserved family vacation

Mary's grandmother with her twin great-grandsons

Mary strikes a casual pose

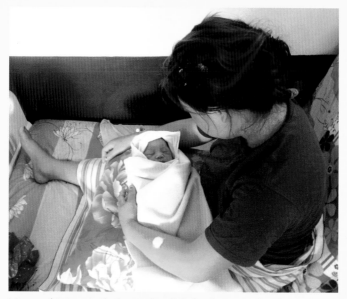

Mary and Prince in the hospital, and (below) Mary and Onler with their three children

(Right) Chungthanglen, or Prince as he is called at home, the new light in Mary's life

Mary and Onler in Delhi with Onler's father some time before he was assassinated

(sitting, L-R) Anu, Cindy (Mary's youngest sister), Mary with one of the twins, Singlenei
(standing, L-R), Onler, Apa with one of the twins, Nengneihat (Mary's first student), Khupreng

Apa, Mangte Tonpa Kom, and Anu, Saneikham Kom

Sandeep Jajodia, chairman and managing director, Monnet Ispat & Energy Limited, felicitating Golden Girl Mary Kom on winning the Bronze at the London Olympics 2012

At the 6th ASBC Asian Women's Boxing Championships, Ulaanbaatar, Mongolia

Mary Kom at the felicitation ceremony-cum-press conference by her sponsors, the Monnet Group

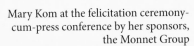

Merciless: at the National Championships 2011 in Bhopal

Mary is a firm teacher and demands the attention and concentration of her students

All kitted up for an informal photo shoot session

Mary's early-morning run with her students is quite a local sight

While she doesn't have a formal coaching degree, Mary has a wealth of experience to share with the students at the academy

A few images from Mary Kom's brush with glitz and glamour. Here, she smiles for the camera with actor Parineeti Chopra

With Prabhu Deva, actor, director, choreographer and the original dancing sensation

A warm hug from Sushmita Sen

And a smile for actor Imran Khan

With actor Dia Mirza

Mary Kom walking the ramp in a Manish Malhotra creation for the charity fashion show in aid of the NGO Mijwan

Mary can more than hold a tune, as her friends and colleagues will tell you

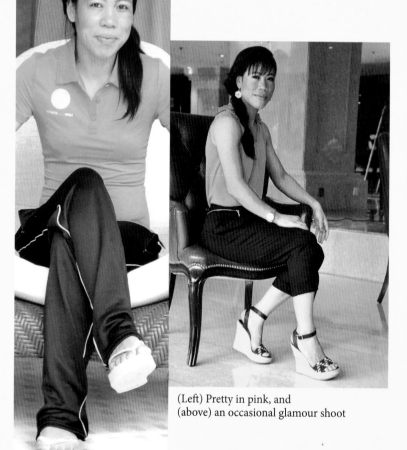

(Left) Pretty in pink, and (above) an occasional glamour shoot

After Christmas Onler and I returned to Imphal on 27 December. As we were relaxing over a cup of tea, the phone rang: unknown insurgents had kidnapped my father-in-law. He had just stepped out of the house to collect coal for the meiphu, a traditional heater that's used in every Manipuri home during the winters. An eyewitness later told us that some men walked up to him and asked him to follow them for a talk. For a while, no one noticed his absence. When the family finally realized he was gone, an alarm was raised and the whole village turned up to search for him. Because there was no electricity in the villages (there still isn't), it was dark everywhere. The frantic search yielded no results. There was a forest right next to the village and insurgents found it easy to wreak havoc and escape into it. Later that night, my father-in-law was found dead some distance away. To this day we do not know who killed him. That there was no demand for money or any other kind of intimation from the insurgents made the whole situation even more painful and frustrating for us.

By the time we reached the village, he had already been found dead. The shock and grief we felt then is beyond anything I have the capacity to describe. Onler was devastated. Till then, it had never occurred to us that we would ever be directly affected by the political problems of our state. These sorts of things always happened to other people. It was a while before the reality, that we were the victims of insurgency, actually sunk in. Friends and relatives started pouring in. New Year's Day was bleak. It remains the most painful chapter in our lives.

At the funeral people came to pay their respects. We were insecure and afraid. Who were the killers? Why did they kill him? What did they want? Would they come again? We stayed in the village until 2007 dawned cold and bitter, and then returned to Imphal. My presence there was worrying Onler no end. I couldn't help but wonder whether my success and popularity had anything to do with my father-in-law's death. It was an anguishing thought. I even considered giving up boxing altogether.

Back in Imphal, Onler's grief gave way to anger. He wanted revenge. We hardly ate. We couldn't sleep. All we could think about was the killing. Onler's refrain was, 'I will avenge my father's death, even if it means joining the insurgency. An eye for an eye. As a man, as a son, I will find the culprits somehow.'

A few of his friends offered to help him get a .32 gun, so that he could take down the killer with the same weapon that his father had been murdered with. I tried all I could to pacify him but his mind was made up. He was tormented day and night. To me it was clear that he was losing his sanity. Boxing now seemed like something in the distant past. I couldn't relate to that life any more. But again, there was a twist of fate, a miracle that changed everything.

8

A new beginning

The days after the killing passed in a haze. I was occupied with consoling my husband and our family, while silently grieving on my own. I was so preoccupied that I had no time to think about myself or my health. I felt sick and nauseous most of the time. I put it down to the stress we were all facing, but Onler, concerned as ever, took me to a doctor. That's how I found out that I was pregnant. We had no plans to start a family so soon. I told my mother first. And then I tried to wrap my head around what had happened. I had to start caring for my health and stop doing any form of vigorous exercise.

Something snapped in Onler's head. He felt all his hair standing up. He felt all his bitterness melting away. He felt like a ray of light had penetrated the dark and gloom of his life. Thoughts of revenge were replaced by thoughts of his unborn child. His very mindset changed: revenge would not bring his father back, and so it was better to forgive and seek divine blessings for his child. The anger was washed away by the hope and joy that the news of my pregnancy brought him.

The friends who were all set to aid him in his revenge were dumbfounded by the change they saw.

So magical was the news of my pregnancy that Onler couldn't help but wonder if we would have twins. His father had been one of a pair of twins. The next medical examination was due for when I was six months pregnant. Meanwhile, everyone commented on the size of my stomach. I would joke, 'Don't you know there are two inside?' But we were worried and thought it best to check with the doctor. After an ultrasound and medical examination, I went out and whispered to my husband, 'We're having twins.' For him, it was like the rebirth of his father. The few dark clouds that still hovered disappeared with that news.

There's another odd story here. I love gardening and in my leisure time I would tend to the small kitchen garden at the back of my house. A pumpkin plant grew there, spreading out all over the backyard. The strange thing was that the plant bore only two identical pumpkins during my pregnancy. Later I would think that it was announcing the arrival of my twins.

As the date for the delivery drew nearer, Onler and I grew agitated. Would anything go wrong? Would it be a normal delivery? If anything, he was more worried than I was. The last month was very tiring for me. With my enormous, heavy stomach, I found it difficult to sleep or lie down.

In my ignorance, I thought that labour pains would be some sort of a stomach ache. That's what I had gathered from seeing women in the village. So when my water broke, I didn't realize that I was already in labour. My back was hurting terribly. I told my husband about it, but he was as ignorant as I was. Since it was night time already, he said he would wait until the morning and call my gynaecologist. He was uneasy though, and tried calling his aunt, who was a nurse.

We couldn't get through to her and so we settled down for the night, still blissfully ignorant of the urgency of the situation. I spent a sleepless night. The next morning, Onler called my gynaecologist, who yelled, 'Bring her at once!' We rushed to the nursing home, reaching around 7 a.m. The doctor took my husband aside and told him that because the water had broken so many hours ago and because of the fluid loss, I needed to have a caesarean surgery. She explained that a normal delivery was possible, but that it was safe for only one child, not two.

I was very worried at the thought of an operation. I wanted to continue boxing after my children were born and an operation might put an end to my chances. Even at that moment, my thoughts were on boxing. I found myself unable to decide one way or the other. For Onler too, it was a difficult moment. He had promised me that he would support my sporting career even after the birth of the twins. What if a caesarean meant that I couldn't play again? My Olympic dream was still unfulfilled. But our aunts and elders who had gathered there were unequivocal in their decision: life was more important than sport. With Onler's approval, I was prepared for surgery. Dr Purnima performed the operation and delivered my twins on 5 August 2007. We were parents to two beautiful, identical baby boys. Another milestone added to the long list against my name.

Life wasn't the same after the twins. The house bustled with people and activity. Relatives of every hue – uncles, aunts, grand-uncles, grand-aunts, cousins – came from far and wide to bless them, shower love on them and look after them. Onler and I soon forgot what it meant to sleep through the night.

I had decided from the very beginning that I would nurse the babies, even if it meant delaying my return to boxing. For the first year of their lives, my only focus was the care of my boys, feeding them, bathing and changing them, carrying them. My husband commented that I was the perfect mother, and that he hadn't expected a boxer to carry a baby so gently, or care for him so expertly. While I glowed with all the praise, the work was really tiring me out. So Onler took over the job of changing their nappies and feeding them at night. When one of the twins was hungry and cried, the other one would follow suit. Onler would feed them both Lactogen. There was no electricity at night, so he'd be groping for the hot water flask in the dark. In his half-asleep state, he knocked over many a flask. Eventually, though, the babies would be changed, fed and lulled back to sleep. Onler was an extraordinarily graceful night-time parent.

Soon enough, it was time to name the babies. In our community, this is a serious affair, in which the opinions of our elders and the heads of our families are sought. My father, my eldest brother-in-law, Paominlen, and other elders got together with us for what turned out to be an exciting, thought-provoking session.

Father came up with the idea of adding 'world' to their names – 'Worldthang' or 'Worldchung' – in honour of my World Championship titles. My parents refer to all World Championship titles as 'World Cup' titles. So the word 'world' is dear to my father. This is not an uncommon practice in my part of the world. It wasn't unusual for children in the village to be named after a significant event or a prized possession of the family. For instance, I remember this one kid who was named 'Cyclethang' after his father bought a cycle – probably the most expensive property they owned. But in the case of my sons, the other elders vetoed my father's idea.

Finally, the elders agreed upon names that were derived from those of the two grandfathers. The elder twin was named 'Rengchungvar', derived from my father-in-law's name, 'Rekhupthang'. The younger twin was 'Khupneivar', which came from my father's name, 'Pontinkhup'.

For a year-and-a-half after the delivery, I stayed with my children, slowly getting my health and strength back, and being the mother that they needed at that age. At some point during this time, Onler asked me what I would do when I retired from boxing. I knew the answer right away: 'I will teach children boxing.' He liked the idea very much. In fact, he's the one who suggested that I should start thinking about setting up an academy to teach the younger generation boxing. The idea stayed with me.

Coincidentally, during my two-year break, no major international tournaments were held.

By the grace of God, there were no complications after my surgery, and I recovered quickly. In fact, quick recovery is one of my strong points. Six months after the delivery, I had started to exercise and build up my stamina again. The doctor had advised me to rest for three years, but two were more than I could handle. I was ready for a comeback a year after the caesarean operation.

9

The comeback

My success, my marriage, the children, all of this was grist for the gossip mills in the village and outside. When I was getting married, everyone cautioned me against it. Afterwards, they all said that I would lose steam and ambition. When I didn't, they made hurtful remarks about my in-laws: 'Look at them. With Mary as their daughter-in-law, their fortune has changed. They are wearing expensive shoes and clothes.' Then, when the babies arrived, they said, this is the end. Even my parents felt that my performance was bound to suffer. All of this hurt and upset me enormously. I wanted to prove them all wrong.

In fact, after the children arrived, Apa had said, 'Sanahen, now that you're a mother, it's enough. You will be tired. Stop boxing. You have won so much, earned enough, and you have a job. You have achieved enough.' Those were good words from a father, but I took them badly. With every international medal, the Ministry of Youth Affairs and Sports gave me money incentives. With the Arjuna Award, I got a prize money of Rs 3.5 lakh. In 2005, I got a job that gave me a monthly income and I was given a house. Apa believed that all of this was more than enough. I had already bought him a paddy field, my siblings' education was taken care of. I was also taking care of my older brother-in-law James's four children too.

Apa thought I had done enough and needed to rest. He kept worrying than an opponent would accidentally hit me on the stomach during a bout. 'What if the stitches open and cause complications?' he asked. People in the village dread surgery. I told him that I wouldn't let anyone hit me on the stomach and declared vehemently that nobody could stop me from boxing. My father's words added fuel to the fire. I became more determined than ever.

The person who used to encourage me the most was my father-in-law, but he was not around to tide me over this difficult phase. He would playfully say that I should keep boxing for as long as I could 'jump about'. I remember with gratitude that he was supportive when even my own parents thought I should stop. 'Let her play as long as she wants,' he said to my husband.

I've often said that I am not comfortable with delivering speeches. I am most articulate in the boxing ring. With my fists. That is where I express myself best. It was yet another reason why I was itching to go back to my sport.

The twins were only a little over a year old when I left for the training camp that would lead to selections for the Fourth Asian Women's Championships. It was hard to part with them but the thought of never being able to box again gave me the strength to leave. I needed to test myself after my long break. Sure enough, I was sick and in pain through the next few weeks of training. As a nursing mother, separation from my children meant that I had to skip feeding them, because of which I developed mastitis. The first night away from them, the pain was so intense that I was up all night crying. From Delhi, where I had a stopover before travelling to Hisar, I called Onler to tell him about the pain. He asked me to consult a doctor immediately. I called on Dr Rosy, whom both of us knew. She prescribed a painkiller, which made things a little better.

In spite of the pain, I was determined to resume training. That one month in Hisar was the most difficult camp experience I have ever had. On the one hand, I was missing my children like crazy. On the other, my body let me down with all these aches and pains. Half the time, I was sick or nauseous, and only managed to do some of the workouts and a little bit of sparring. The coaches were understanding and did not push me too hard. I endured the camp, getting through it one day at a time. More than once, I had to beat down the yearning to hang up my gloves and run home.

However, the attitude of the other girls, particularly those from my weight category, pushed me to stick it out in the camp. None of them said anything snide, but their looks said it all. They seemed to think my peak performance was behind me, that I was no threat to them any more. My determination saw me through and I was selected for the tournament, which was to be held in Guwahati in September 2008. I was given the honour of taking the oath on behalf of all the participants. I was a little nervous about my comeback, but I also felt centred and positive.

My first fight was the quarter-final bout. When I stepped into the ring, the nervousness fell away. I got back my rhythm. I was down 0–2 in the first round, but in the second, I remained calm and was able to concentrate. I won the match 8–2. It was more than I could have hoped for. I had just come back from a two-year break, with only a two-month camp to re-train my body and mind. God's blessings, my husband's support and the hard work put in by my coaches helped me get there. Onler was in the gallery to witness and cheer my return. He had left the kids back home with my mother.

I wasn't too impressed with my performance in the semi-final bout against Nguyen Thi Hoa of Vietnam, but I managed to win the round and qualify for the final, where I had to face Jong Ok of North Korea. I had defeated her earlier, in the Third Women's World Championships in Russia, but on this occasion, I couldn't. I had to settle for silver.

For Apa, it was proof that his doomsday predictions were coming true. 'See, this time you got only a silver. Do you want to end your career in disgrace? Do you want people to backbite and criticize your performance? You should have stopped when you were at the top.' I was enraged, and told him that I was perfectly happy with a silver after a two-year break and very little practice. I could talk to Apa and explain my decision. To stop the other tongues wagging, I had to better my performance and prove them wrong. I would show him and everyone else what I was capable of, I resolved.

I took a two-week break and went home. The twins had grown bigger. I couldn't take my eyes off them. I had missed them terribly. But before I had even settled down, it was time to leave again – to Vishakhapatnam this time, for training and selection ahead of the Fifth World Championships. Because I had been so miserable in Hisar, my husband thought it best if I took the twins with me. He felt I would be able to concentrate better if the babies were close by. My mother and a baby-sitter accompanied me and the kids to the camp. This was quite unusual, and I'm sure I made quite a comical entrance with my entourage.

A training camp is a physically demanding space, with exercises, sparring, shadow-boxing and the like in the mornings and evenings. In between all of that, I was feeding the boys. At night, I would tend to them. They were unused to the hot weather and were especially restless. I was exhausted. My team-mates were surprised that I managed to wake up early for the morning training. The girls did come by and visit the boys and hold them, but none of them could help in any way, because they were as busy as I was with the training schedule. It was draining but the flipside was that I could see them and hold them. It was in Vishakhapatnam that my sons began to crawl for the first time – a development I would have missed if I had left them behind. I was very excited. But their newfound mobility brought with it its own set of problems. They tried to crawl everywhere, even falling off the bed. Mother still says about those days, 'Oh! It was so difficult to take care of the twins in the hot weather.'

Through all of this, Onler held fort at home. He was in constant touch with us and missed the twins, but couldn't come and join us because of all the things that needed attention at home. Onler knew from the very beginning that he had to give up on his studies and career to help me further my sporting career. With my steady success came a range of problems. He felt that I needed someone to push me all the time and he wanted to be that someone. Right after our marriage, Onler was involved with an NGO, but after the birth of our twins, he had to give that up too. Apart from taking care of the children, and everything at home, Onler now also handled my career, leaving me free to concentrate on my game. In Manipur, men do not do the work of women. It's frowned upon. But Onler handled everything during my near-constant absence. A man holding a broom or doing household work is labelled 'henpecked' and spoken of disparagingly – but Onler was unaffected. He has always had a core of quiet strength in him. I too draw support and strength from it.

The first thing I needed to work on after my comeback was fitness. The training patterns hadn't changed in all the years that I had been boxing. I felt that the techniques we used were outdated when compared to what I had seen in other countries. We did not even have a dietician to monitor our food and fitness.

Fortunately, by this time I had a sponsor, and through them a specialist doctor was assigned to me. She advised me to increase my calcium intake, since I had given birth. Earlier, all I ate was my usual food, with fruits, glucose and vitamins. In the village, no one spoke about health and dietary matters, so I had no idea that I was supposed to eat a certain sort of food and take supplements to recover from the effects of childbirth. After I had my twins, even a few bouts would exhaust me. Apart from my natural resilience, the reason I managed to get back on the right track so quickly was the attention I got in terms of nutrition, physical health and better training.

I thought it would help to have foreign coaches to keep up with the competition. I had worked with Indian coaches for over a decade, and by now I was itching to learn new techniques and tactics that boxers in other countries were learning. But until boxing became an Olympic sport, that would not be a priority for my training.

After my defeat in the Asian Championship finals, I worked harder on every aspect of my game. I gave thought to my overall regimen: the right food supplements, rigorous training, and working up the confidence I needed. I went on to win gold at the Ninth Senior Women's National Championships held in Agra in November 2008. That was a boost before I headed to my next destination: the Fifth World Championships in Ningbo, China, later that month.

Ningbo was amazing. We stayed right in the middle of the city and were surrounded by shops and malls. It was the first time I actually had money to shop with. I took Rs 50,000 with me and bought many things, even a camcorder for myself. As for the tournament itself, I was feeling fairly confident because I was familiar with the players. My opponent in the finals was my old rival, the Romanian, Steluta Duta. I was not worried initially, but then it occurred to me that I should never take an opponent lightly. So I declined invitations to the guided tours and instead spent my time practising and exercising. The effort paid off.

In a repeat of the fourth edition of the championship in Delhi, I defeated Steluta Duta 7–1 in the final. It was, as I remember it, a pretty one-sided match. For me, it was a historic fourth gold. I retained my title and became the most successful woman boxer in the world.

Women's boxing was picking up by then, and the competition was getting tougher. Many countries had women's boxing teams now and were participating with increasing fervour. In that sense, the fifth edition of the championship was significant. But my hard work and willpower helped me overcome odds that critics said I could not face. In a country starved for success in international competitions, I became the most successful athlete.

Of the four gold medals I secured in the World Championships, this was the most precious. It was distilled from all the sacrifices I had made. Leaving my husband behind was bad enough, but parting from the twins was heartbreaking. I missed many milestones of their growing up. I left them for a camp or a tournament to come back and find them bigger, their faces just a little different. This medal was for them.

With the fourth world title, I got a promotion in the state police department – to the post of inspector.

Things began to come easily to me. But it was not so long ago that I had to fight for every bit of recognition. It was a recognition I sought not only for myself, but for my sport and, even more specifically, for women's boxing. My first gold at a world championship had put me in contention for the Arjuna Award. But my name had been struck off at the last moment. It had been a personal disappointment, and I knew that an Arjuna for me would have meant recognition that women's boxing was being treated at par with other sports.

The award finally came to me on 21 September 2004. My father travelled with me to Delhi to receive it. I had been provided with a sari and a blazer for the function, and was required to wear a matching blouse. The hitch was that I had never worn a sari in my life. Fortunately, the friendly staff at the Ashoka Hotel helped me. It took us almost half an hour to get it right. They ensured it was pinned up in strategic places so I didn't trip over it and make a fool of myself. Interestingly, at the Asian Games 2010 opening ceremony in China, it turned out that none of my team-mates in the boxing team knew how to wear a sari and I was the one helping them wrap theirs, gathering what I could remember from my Arjuna Award sari-draping experience.

Soon after the Arjuna, in 2005, I was selected for the Padma Shri, the country's fourth-highest civilian award. With that, I felt my contribution to raising the profile of the sport was finally being recognized.

However, in 2009, the prestigious Rajiv Gandhi Khel Ratna award, the highest sporting honour in India, came to me with a history of some acrimony. My application was rejected the first time. The way it works is that the athlete applies through the state government's Department of Youth Affairs and Sports with a recommendation from the Indian Boxing Federation. The second time the IBF forwarded my name, Milkha Singh of the selection committee struck it off, saying he didn't know which sport I competed in. I felt so humiliated by that comment that I responded publicly with this question: 'How many more titles do I have to win for the country to believe I deserve the honour?'

But how could I beat the cricketers? M.S. Dhoni won the award after one World Cup win. The then sports minister, M.S. Gill, assured me that I would be given justice. It was a balm that soothed my anger. Finally it was announced that Vijender Singh, bronze medallist boxer in the Beijing Olympics, Sushil Kumar, bronze medallist in wrestling at the same Olympics, and I would jointly receive the award. In a glittering ceremony at Rashtrapati Bhavan on 29 August 2009, I received the award from President Pratibha Patil. My appearance on stage was greeted with thunderous applause. It was a dream-like feeling. The award included a citation and prize money of Rs 7.5 lakh. Sitting in the Rashtrapati Bhavan with all those renowned sportspeople around me, I felt my spirit and my commitment to my country's sporting glory renewed. I dedicated the award to my sons who were still too young to understand why their mother kept leaving them and going away. I hoped they would understand one day.

The Khel Ratna paved the way for other things as well. The

corporate world started to come forward to sponsor individual sports. Their involvement helped the sport in general, as well as me personally, because of the increased resources available for equipment and travel, as well as investment in new ways of looking at health and training.

There was also the fact that I was not always recognized as Indian in my own country. Because of our oriental looks, people from the Northeast are often mocked in other parts of India. We're called Nepalis, or Chinkies, and people call us names like ching-ching chong-chong. In a country where people speak all kinds of languages and have varied kinds of looks, why is such treatment meted out to us? When I used to say that I am from Manipur, many people didn't even know where it was. To be honest, in Manipur too we refer to people from mainland India as 'Mayangs', or non-Manipuri, and that too makes me sad.

Whether or not I look 'Indian', I am Indian and I represent India, with pride and all my heart. Often, when I travelled abroad, the Chinese, Korean, Mongolian, Vietnamese or Thai athletes would mistake me for one of their own. Each time, I would explain that I was Indian. But you look like us, not like them, they would say, pointing at my team-mates.

After so many years of dominating the world championships, I have become a familiar face to boxers from other countries, as well as to people in my own country. I hope the coverage in many leading magazines will open the minds of our people about the Northeast. Sport has always been a uniting force, in India and around the world. It has enabled me to know so much, learn and see so much of my country and the world. I am proud when mediapersons from across the world come to Kangathei to trace the story of women's boxing. I feel I have played a big part in making that happen.

10

The operation

When I returned to boxing, I had made my peace with the fact that motherhood would have to take a backseat for a few years. The most difficult part of this was hearing the occasional news that my sons were unwell, even if it was only a slight fever or a runny nose. My husband would often just not tell me, to keep me from worrying. But someone or the other would mention something, and then I would be mad at Onler for hiding these details about my boys' well being from me. I tried to reason with him and told him that even if I couldn't be with them, as their mother, I had a right to know. At least I could pray for them.

Both of us are hot-tempered, so many of these conversations would end in tiffs. 'Don't call me any more,' I would tell him. Since he cools off quicker than I do, he would say calmly, 'If I tell you, you will only think of home and the children, and your game will suffer.'

The fact is that it was possible for me to go out and focus on my boxing only because of Onler. Many times, we had sponsorship for my husband to accompany me on my travels abroad. However much he was tempted, he would always decline the offer, because the children were too small to be left solely in the care of others. He couldn't bear the thought of the children sleeping separately in a nursery, so they slept with him. Onler complains that for three years after they were born, he didn't know what a proper night's sleep was like.

The children were often the reason for our petty quarrels. I tend to be stern with them, and they are so naughty and disobedient that I give them a little beating now and then. My husband gets really angry when I do that. He is worried that I may forget my own strength and hit them harder than I intend to. Of course, if he decides to punish them, then I am the one that's upset. On the whole, though, the task of disciplining our children and teaching them the right values is left to Onler, because I am away most of the time. It is a measure of my faith in him that this does not worry me at all.

The greatest challenge I had to confront in my boxing career was the news of my younger son's illness just before the 2011 Asian Cup in Haikou, China. Rengchungvar (Rengpa) had a cold and a fever, so Onler was taking him to a reputed paediatrician in Imphal. I suggested that he take Khupneivar (Nainai) as well. He didn't see the point, but for some reason, I insisted. Isn't it said that the mother has a special instinct?

The doctor prescribed medicines for Rengpa's cold and fever. But what he revealed about Nainai came as a shock: there was something wrong with his heartbeat. Further investigations revealed that he had a hole in his heart. He was a normal three-year-old boy who had never shown any symptoms of sickness. We were shattered. Onler and I decided to take him to Chandigarh for treatment; we had friends there, so it would be easier for us. We consulted Dr

T. Shyam K. Singh at the Postgraduate Institute of Medical Education and Research. Just a few days before the Asia Cup, the doctor told us to admit Nainai for surgery.

I decided not to go for the competition, but my family members, and especially Onler, insisted that I do. He assured me that he would take care of everything, and that there was little I could do anyway because the date of the operation had not been finalized.

I went to China with the team, but my heart was heavy. Onler called every day with updates and to tell me that Nainai was fine. He assured me that the surgery would take place after I returned. I prayed fervently, cast my fears aside and focused on the game. I was away from my family during one of our most trying times. I had to make the effort pay off. I did – I won the gold. While the team was celebrating, I was itching to be back in Chandigarh.

We reached Delhi late at night. Fortunately, my sponsors, IOS, had arranged for me to travel to Chandigarh as soon as I set foot in Delhi. I reached just in time to see my son being wheeled into the operation theatre. He was very happy to see me. I accompanied him as far as the door, and assured him that I would wait right outside for him. With a prayer, I let go of his hand. The surgery went on for a long time. We sat outside, barely breathing, praying as hard as we could. Finally, the doors of the theatre opened and my son was wheeled out with lots of tubes attached to his tiny body. He was in the ICU for three days, during which time I kept vigil by his side on a stool, my head resting on the wall behind.

The moment Nainai regained consciousness, he looked for me. I had to be near him round the clock. The moment I stepped out for something, he would start yelling for me and pulling out the tubes and needles that were attached to his body. He was discharged after a long stay, hale and hearty, with no damage except for a scar. We call it the Spiderman scar. He's a normal five-year-old who runs and jumps around with his brother. At times I have to scold them and tell them to be careful, because they don't realize the implications of going through a major heart surgery.

Soon after we returned home, it was time to travel again. My boys would ask, 'One night or two nights?' By now they are used to seeing me leave. Of course, I still need to pacify them each time and promise to bring back toys of their choice. Sometimes they ask direct questions like, 'Mummy, why do you go far away and leave us?'

My younger son is more attached to me. When I am home, he keeps coming to check on me every now and then to make sure that I am home. Rengpa is more independent. Between the two of them, it's like there's a permanent hurricane in the house. They love to draw – on their books, the walls, everywhere. They've just learnt to spell their names, so it's everywhere, even outside the gates.

I'm often asked about my travels and my favourite places. If I were to answer truly, I'd have to say, home – with my children. That's where and when I'm the happiest. Everywhere I go, I like to speak for the rights of children. They are our hope for the future and our surest source of joy today.

11

And then again

In September 2010, I went to Barbados to compete in the Sixth World Boxing Championships. It was my sixth participation, with a medal to mark each one, a silver in the first and golds thereafter. It had been a long journey – ten years long, beginning in Kangathei and going all the way to Bridgetown, Barbados.

My weight category, 46 kg, was no longer recognized by the AIBA, and so I would be competing in the 48 kg slot. Although I had started out at 48 kg in the first championship in Pennsylvania, I had moved down to 45 kg by the second one, and then gone up to 46 kg for the Second Asian Women's Boxing Championships in Hisar in 2003. Until 2008, this was the category I fought in.

However, I was confident that my experience and the increased training after childbirth would carry me through. Also, it was a lucky thing that many of my opponents were actually 46 kg fighters who had to move to a higher category, like I did. So my opponents were more or less the boxers I would have faced in my regular weight category. Of course, in the new category, there were some who were taller and stronger than I, but the difference was not so great that I really felt the strain. My years of training and experience stood me in good stead here. Apart from my own natural aggression, the one quality I have is the ability to think quickly. I look, observe my opponent's techniques, think and then fight.

Once again, in the final bout, I was up against Steluta Duta, my old rival. Steluta played hard, and ended the first round 4–3 ahead. But the second round was all mine. I landed a well-timed hit and evened out our scores. Steluta didn't quite recover her pace after that. By the end of that round, I was leading 9–5, and by the end of the third I had reached 12–5. I could see the gold now well within my grasp, so I gave the last round everything I had, winning the bout 16–6.

My husband was awake and tracking the scores of the match online until late into the night. I called him up to tell him. It was a very emotional conversation. Only he knew what I had gone through to clinch this medal.

When I returned to Manipur, thousands of people had lined up at the airport complex. Enthusiastic crowds spilled out on to the streets as we drove into the city. I was taken in an open jeep straight to the Khuman Lampak Indoor Stadium, where the chief minister, O. Ibobi Singh, was the chief guest. Several other ministers and high-ranking officials also attended the ceremony. The chief minister handed me an incentive award of Rs 10 lakh and announced that I had been promoted to Additional Superintendent of Police. Once again, he proposed that the road leading to the Langol Games Village be renamed 'M.C. Mary Kom Road'. Nothing has come of this yet.

Speeches followed, and I was overwhelmed to hear words

of praise and support from all these important people in Manipur. I recalled my days of struggle and expressed the desire to set up a boxing academy and train students for the future. It was a thought that had stayed with me since I had children of my own, and Onler and I had discussed it as something I should do in the future. I thanked the government, and particularly the chief minister, for the encouragement. I said I was proud to be Manipuri and to represent Manipur. I ended by expressing my gratitude to the people of the state and to my well-wishers, and with the hope that I could win a gold at the Olympics.

Yes, after all these years of boxing, I finally had a chance to take part in the Olympic Games, the greatest event in the world of sport. Women's boxing had been recognized and was going to be part of the 2012 Games in London. That was always my dream and now, in a year and some months, I was going to take part in the Olympics.

The sports minister, M.S. Gill, too sent a note of congratulations, saying, 'She has an exceptional record. Manipur has great sports talent and Mary Kom is the best.'

It was balm to my soul to hear all that praise. During training and selection camps, I was always one of a bunch of players. I had to prove myself over and over, regardless of my track record. There were many players in my weight category from Haryana, Manipur, Delhi and other states. During the trials for every selection there would be tough competition among us. But I would retain focus and determination until I had my spot.

There is one particular incident I remember when I lost my cool. During the sparring sessions, I was sometimes made to fight four rounds with different opponents with a 30-second rest in between. This was something the coaches asked of all players, so they could test our strength and build up our stamina. Once, during such a sparring session in Delhi, the small gym was packed with far too many players. I was feeling so hot and tired that I lost my cool and took off my gloves, saying I wouldn't play any more. While everyone had to spar, I did sometimes feel that I was marked, made to fight continuously to deliberately tire me. But I fought with a do-or-die attitude. It wasn't easy to keep me down.

Someone once said that when Mary boxes, she hits her opponents bop-bop-bop; that's exactly what I do. My selections have been purely on the basis of my performances, not because of my previous medals or past glory. Even the Olympic berth, which came my way under controversial circumstances, was something I fought for like a tigress.

Back home, my family and I celebrated joyously. It was sweet success. We offered our thanks to God and I prayed for success at the Olympics.

12

The highs and lows

Before I talk about the Olympic Games and the fulfilment of a childhood dream, I want to stop and reflect on the sport of boxing and its administration in our country. I discussed in an earlier chapter the politics that plagued the Manipur boxing scenario. The national milieu was no better.

In the beginning, when women's boxing was not yet an established discipline, there was no politicking. Training camps were held in various parts of India, and coaches from different states attended them, wards in tow. The atmosphere was one of camaraderie and solidarity. Juniors would seek the advice of seniors, who would gladly help. In those years, everyone was working towards a common goal: to develop women's boxing as a respectable sport in India, and to work towards its inclusion in the Olympic Games.

In October 2002, ahead of the Antalya World Championships, twenty-five girls were training at the Nehru Stadium in New Delhi. We were being coached by National Coach Anoop Kumar and his assistant. Anoop sir found no time to work with me. Upset, I took off my gloves and gear and sat in one corner. He was forced to come and coax me to train, and even promised me a flight ticket back if I brought home a gold. Such was the closeness we shared with our coaches in the early days.

I am going to talk about the more difficult aspects of my boxing career now, but before I do that, I would like to state clearly that none of this impacts the respect and gratitude that I feel for my coaches over the years at the many national camps I have attended. Every one of them – Mahavir Singh, Bhaskar Bhatt, Hemlata Badwal, Venkateswara Rao, Ajit Kumar Singh, Sagar Dhayal, D. Chandra Lal – has contributed to making me the boxer I am today.

Still, there is no gainsaying the fact that, over the last five years or so, there has been a dramatic change. One of the measures taken to maximize the impact of training camps is to divide us into groups, each of which is placed under different coaches. While this is an efficiency measure, in effect it encourages groupism and favouritism among both the students and the coaches. Quite often, when training starts, the atmosphere is about as tense as it is at some disputed international border. Needless to say, this affects the performance of our athletes.

Even back in 2001, when things were much more friendly, there were accusations of nepotism. Oja Narjit had accused the IABF of 'readymade selections' to the First Asian Women's Boxing Championships to be held in Bangkok. Of the ten girls on his team, seven were selected. He said that the three left out were better than those selected. Being a boxer from the Northeast, and particularly from a remote region in Manipur, I was always worried about being dropped from the selections. Because of this, I never once let my guard down in any sporting event or space.

I am never going to forget the Senior National Women's Boxing camp in Jamshedpur in 2009. In my quarter-final fight against Pinky Jangra from Haryana, our points tied at 15–15 in the 46 kg flyweight category. The verdict went in favour of Pinky. Anil Bohidar, senior joint secretary of the IABF, said the judges had declared Pinky the winner because her technique, defence and style were better. I agree it was a close fight, but their declaration that her technique and style were better broke my heart. I felt my years of seniority and past performance ought to have weighed in on the judges' decision. I registered a protest, and they suspended me for 'unsporting' behaviour. I still hold the view that I lost because there was lobbyism at work, or rather that Pinky won the match due to a bias that worked in her favour.

The decision to suspend me was taken by a nine-judge jury headed by N.S. Kichi, vice-president of the IABF. I was not even officially aware of the twenty-two-day suspension. My husband informed me after reading reports in the press. I demanded a rematch to prove myself and submitted a petition to P.K. Muralidharan Raja, secretary, IABF. After a meeting with him, I decided to apologize for my unsporting behaviour and the temporary suspension was revoked. I was humiliated and hurt but I decided to bide my time.

That time came in the Twelfth National Championships in 2011 in Bhopal at the Tatya Tope Stadium. I had increased my weight category to 51 kg, the minimum at the Olympics (in 2009, women's boxing was officially announced as being part of the Games in 2012). In the finals of the National Championships, I was to face Pinky, who had defeated Sarita in a close, much-talked-about bout. Pinky won on an individual judge's score, as the tally was locked at 34–all after four rounds of intense battle. First round, they were evenly matched at 7 each. In the second round, Sarita took the lead 11–10, in the third round, they each had 9 points. In the final round, Pinky took the lead 8–7 and was declared winner.

Meanwhile, I was ready to get my own back. With all my supporters, including my father, to cheer me on, I defeated her 13–9. When reporters asked me about my earlier bout, I blurted out: 'If a world-class player is defeated by a national player because of the judges' decision, it means things are not on track.'

As an aside, after the match, many parents brought their children to me. They asked for my autograph, some touched my feet. My father was shocked. 'Mary,' he said, 'you are not God. Why are you letting them worship you? At least don't allow them to touch your feet!' I calmed him, saying, 'Apa, don't bother. They won't stop even if I tell them to.' Having never seen it before, he found the gesture very strange.

By this time, the International Olympic Committee (IOC) had declared the inclusion of women's boxing in the 2012 Games. Only three weight categories were included: 51 kg flyweight, 57 to 60 kg lightweight and 69 to 75 middle weight. The Olympic camp was scheduled to begin at the Netaji Subhas National Institute of Sports (NIS), Patiala, which has one of the best facilities for boxing in India.

Two coaches, both Dronacharya awardees – Damodaran Chandra Lal from Kerala and Anoop Kumar from Haryana – were entrusted with coaching the women boxers. I had spent some of my best years training with coach Anoop, who is chief coach of women's boxing. Unfortunately, the two coaches were pitted against each other – largely because the boxers had started to lobby for teaming up with the coach of their choice.

I happened to be placed in Anoop Kumar's group, while

Sarita was included in Chandra Lal's group. Right from the beginning of my days in boxing, Sarita and I had been bosom-friends. We shared everything, including conversations about personal and family matters. But since the Asian Games 2010 selections, there had been a growing rift between us. (I will come to this in some detail later, because I know that it has been a matter of speculation among viewers and boxers alike.)

There was talk of a new chief coach being appointed, and rumours were that it would Chandra Lal. My view, as a senior boxer, was sought on this issue, and I said that a new chief coach just before the Olympics would destabilize the team. If a new coach had been selected two or three years earlier, according to proper protocol, it would not have been a problem. I met the sports minister and senior boxing officials to campaign against the move. The result was that Kumar continued as chief coach. Meanwhile, I moved on to thinking about a strategy for my training.

My coaches back in Manipur had equipped me with a strong grasp of the basics of boxing. The only thing I lacked back at home was strong enough competition to practice against and hone my skills. This is where training camps and bouts with international players helped – they broadened my horizon.

While there were talented women boxers from states like Mizoram, Assam, Bengal, Bihar and Kerala, the most talented in terms of tactics and tricks are the Haryana girls. My coaches had only taught me the rules of boxing and the right techniques and styles. I had no other tricks up my sleeve. My teammates from Manipur and I had been told to be disciplined, avoid injury and respect the rules. However, as I gained experience, I encountered players who used various tricks and it agitated me. I have always been aggressive in the ring. I would fight back using the same tricks; I am an eye-for-an-eye kind of girl. One trick was to hold an opponent and throw her, like wrestlers do. Another was to hit an opponent on the head swiftly while clinging – as her arms are pinned down, she cannot use them to attack. In an exhibition bout in a camp in Haryana during my early boxing days, I got injured when my opponent suddenly hit me with her head. I got a cut on my left eyelid and needed stitches. But I wised up to these tricks fairly quickly, giving as good as I got. I've never suffered any major injury in my career, just minor scratches and bruises.

I don't like talking about the Indian women's boxing scenario in terms of state teams, but that is the reality of how things operate on the ground. Even during training, I was often neglected and not given enough attention by the coaches. When coaches and other boxing officials favoured their own state players, the only way I could fight back was in the ring, and by aiming higher and higher. That's why, even with the odds against me, after the shift to the higher weight category, I knew that I would fight to the finish for an Olympic berth – and then, for an Olympic gold.

13

The countdown

Everyone who knows me will confirm that I was single-mindedly focused on the Olympics ever since I found out that women's boxing would be a part of the Games in London 2012. I have always felt that the reason I have done so well is because every time I enter the ring, I tell myself, 'I must win. I will fight to win.' I take every tournament seriously and aim to win every bout. But in my heart I hoped that every one of those bouts, those fights, were training me for the Olympics. Even during my two-year break, I followed women's boxing closely. I kept waiting for news that women's boxing would be recognized as an Olympic sport. It had become an obsession. When I heard that women's boxing would be excluded from the Athens Olympics, my heart sank. In four years, I would be older, less fit perhaps. And women boxers across the world were disappointed at the short shrift we were given by the Olympic Games organizers.

As brand ambassador of the AIBA, my performance was highlighted in the campaign to include women's boxing in the

Olympics. Before the IOC meeting, I had said, 'Boxing is my career, my life. I'm just hoping that IOC will give us female boxers the perfect answer.' Our prayers and hard work paid off. Women boxers would be able to participate in the 2012 Olympics in London. IOC President Jacques Rogge said in a press release on 13 August 2009, 'AIBA welcomes women to the world of Olympic boxing following today's historic decision by the International Olympic Committee to include women's boxing from the 2012 Olympic Games in London.' A good share of this credit must go to AIBA President Ching-Kuo Wu, who worked hard to get women our due ever since he was elected in 2006. As part of his campaign, he had also highlighted my achievements to the IOC.

And so, I was going to fight the battle of my life: to get an Olympic berth. The boxing ring became a battlefield. The first hurdle was that my weight category was not included in the Olympics, forcing me to increase my weight to 51 kg and gear up to meet bigger and taller opponents.

To this end, participation in the Asian Games 2010 in Guangzhou, China, would be a first step. The Asian Games too had included women's boxing for the first time, with the weight categories 51 kg, 60 kg and 75 kg. The IABF was holding trials for the team that would go to China. IABF Secretary-General Col. Muralidharan offered to shift the dates for me since I had just returned from Barbados. But I wanted no special favours and insisted that I would go on the same day as the others.

This was the greatest challenge of my career and I was going to meet it. As were all the women boxers. My state-mate Sarita, and Haryana boxers Meena Kumari and Pinky Jangra were also eyeing a berth in the 51 kg category. With the coaches, whether from Manipur or Haryana, favouring their own boxers, I knew I was alone in my fight. Comments about my eligibility began flying thick and fast: 'Mary is so small, how can she win?' 'She won't stand a chance against the bigger, stronger boxers in that category' or 'She has fighting spirit and technique, but her height and weight are against her.' I steeled myself to prove them all wrong and prayed to God to keep me calm. There were young and new boxers, but their enthusiasm and youth could not match my experience and my hunger for an Olympic gold. I had waited years and years for this opportunity.

For an Olympic berth, I would need to compete against boxers from five weight categories:

1. Pinweight: 44–46 kg
2. Lightweight: 46–48 kg
3. Flyweight: 48–50 kg
4. Light Bantamweight: 50–52 kg
5. Bantamweight: 52–54 kg

From within these categories would emerge the players that qualified for the 51 kg Olympic flyweight category. Besides my weight, I also needed to up the ante on my power punches. This meant extra weight training and extra food intake. I began to think about asking the sports authorities for a foreign coach.

A selection trial was held for the Asian Games 2010 by the IBF to pick the Indian team. I was up against Sarita for the 51-kg slot. The first trial was held in Bhopal, and there were talks that Sarita had already been selected. But I have a recording of that match and am pretty confident that it ought to have gone in my favour. Later, the decision on the Bhopal match was withheld because the results were inconclusive. It was decided that another match would be held, and both Sarita and I agreed to this. I defeated Sarita in the repeat bout held in Delhi in September, and was selected to go on to the Asian Games. She accused the IBF general secretary of favouritism in the selection. I was told that she said, 'Mary Kom will not get any medal in the 51 kg.' But I was unmoved. I have always had a strong heart and that helps me cope. Criticism only brings out the fighter in me.

I couldn't win a gold at the 16th Asian Games at Guangzhou, China. I went down fighting to China's Ren Cancan 11–7 in the semi-final. I came back with a bronze. Ren Cancan, 5'6" tall, was the AIBA title holder in the 51-kg category at the Barbados World Championships. It was an unfamiliar weight category and the defeat was not entirely unexpected. But I was very disappointed. I was gunning for gold; I always am. Later, I met Cancan again at the Sixth Asian Women's Boxing Championships in 2012. That time, I beat her.

The rapid progress I made was due to my British coach Charles Atkinson, with whom I'd been training since May 2011. I knew that I needed to be proactive. I approached the Sports Ministry and requested them to provide me with a foreign coach. The minister, Ajay Maken, met me and approved my request. My sponsors, Olympic Gold Quest (OGQ), helped me identify the right coach. Charles is a World Boxing Council coach, and was the guiding force behind the rise of Thai male boxers in the 1980s. The only drawback was that he did not have an AIBA three-star certificate, a degree required of an official coach at the Olympics.

Charles's lessons made a huge difference to my fighting style. We concentrated on punches, strength, the guard and combinations. The results were there for all to see. My opponents found it hard to get through my defence. Charles also gave me tips on how to improve my attack and counter-attack with combination punches and jabs. He taught me how to tailor my defences depending on my opponent's boxing style.

OGQ also provided me with top-class infrastructure, including taking care of my travel and stay. More importantly, they ensured that I had the services of physiotherapist Janhavi Jathar to monitor my health and recovery from childbirth. She even stayed with me in Imphal for some time. I began my exercises under her supervision.

I needed the doctor's assistance to increase my weight through the intake of nutrition in a scientific manner. To compete in the 51 kg category, I had to be between 48 and 51 kg. In the lower categories, it's better to be at the higher end of the weight spectrum because every kilo makes a difference to the punch. It took me six months to gain about a kilo-and-a-half. This was quite the opposite for Ren Cancan and Nicola Adams, the two top contenders, who were fighting in the 54-kg slot earlier and were struggling to reduce their weight. They were both taller than me. The other thing I needed to watch out for through my weight gain was to keep the fat off, for that would slow me down.

This was timely intervention. Winning gold at the Sixth Asian Women's Boxing Championships at Mongolia was a huge morale booster. I was now set for the World Championships 2012 in Qinhuangdao, China. This was where boxers would qualify for the London Games. It was, in fact, the *only* qualifying event for the historic debut of women boxers at the Olympics. This time, I had to participate in the 51 kg at the championships and try for a record sixth world title.

I got a bye in the first round, so my first fight was with Ayako Minowa from Japan. She went down 20–9. This was the first time I met her, and it was a very confusing match. Minowa was very strong, but had no skill or technique. She fought like a bull, only hitting my belly. Had I fought like her, we might as well have been fighting on the streets. Instead, I counter-attacked using mostly my left hook, which confused her. The next match was against Marielle Hanson of Norway, whom I defeated 26–16 to move to the quarter-finals. It was a good bout. She was tall and very accurate with her punches. Her technique was neat, allowing me to test all my combination punches without draining me out. Next up was Adams, who had lost to Cancan at Barbados to bag a silver. I had defeated Cancan recently, but I knew that Adams was not one to be taken lightly. I studied her videos intensely to plan my strategy.

On 16 May 2013, I was ready for combat and sent a prayer up to God as I always do. I fought fiercely, using all of my experience and knowledge. I conceded a point each in the first and last rounds, and ultimately lost. Adams won 13–11. I was devastated. It had been such a close fight. And this was the first time ever that I would be going back empty-handed from a World Women's Boxing Championship.

I now waited anxiously for the result of the semi-final between Adams and Russia's Elena Savelyeva. My ticket to the Olympics depended on their fight. Elena had defeated North Korea's Hye Kim and Adams had beaten me. The rule was that if Adams won, the girl she had beaten – me – would qualify, and if Savelyeva won, Hye Kim would go through.

I have never rooted for an opponent the way I did this time. Luck was with me: Adams defeated Savelyeva 11–6.

My team-mates were not so lucky. I felt that I had already created history by becoming the first Indian woman boxer – and the only one that year – to qualify for the Olympics.

My long-desired Olympic medal was almost within reach, I believed. My disappointment at not winning was forgotten in my euphoria at having qualified for the Games.

Earlier, OGQ had organized a month-long training camp at the Balewadi Sports Complex in Pune – a world-class venue. With permission from the Sports Ministry, I trained separately and exclusively there. It was a very different experience. In the national training camps, one coach took charge of more than twenty girls at a time, whereas in Pune I trained alone with handpicked sparring partners. While OGQ organized this, it was done in coordination with the IABF and fully funded by the Sports Ministry.

I began training exclusively at Balewadi from March 2012 onwards. I enjoyed the focused attention I was getting. The weather in Pune was good and the sports complex peaceful. The accommodation was comfortable too. The food was good. When I got bored of spicy curries, I cooked simple food that was more to my taste. I have a taste for boiled vegetables cooked with a hint of seasoning. My very favourite food, in fact, is plain boiled rice with a simple vegetable curry and smoked fish, and hot chutney as a side dish. I was required to eat well and my weight was checked as many as seven times a day. Sadly, after the gruelling exercise and sparring for two or three hours, all the weight I had gained seemed to melt away. But all in all, Balewadi was the ideal place to focus on training.

Altogether, four training camps were conducted. My training partners were from Manipur. MABA agreed to send local training partners, as I'd be able to converse with them more easily, given my language problems. Oja Kishan also came, with the three boys that Onler and I had selected in Manipur. We had checked their height and style of boxing. We were looking for one orthodox, one southpaw and one who was a mix of both. They had to closely resemble my probable opponents in the Olympics and also had to be disciplined boxers, because I could not risk any injury just before the Games. At the last camp my partners came from the junior boys at the Army Sports Institute in Pune. My coach, Charles, and I went to the institute to select the right partners. Just before the Olympics, training sessions were held for four weeks in Pune and two in Liverpool.

Throughout, my association with Charles was very fruitful. While we didn't speak the same language, we did share our faith in Christianity and our passion for boxing. He made me feel secure and cared for. His main focus was on developing my strength and stamina. Boxing is a game of the eyes and feet, but the most important element is stamina. When one has stamina, the hands will automatically hit. Without stamina, a boxing match is easily lost, no matter the skill level. The training exercises at Pune, therefore, were mainly focused on endurance.

I had to run ten rounds of the athletic track, at medium speed to begin with. As my speed increased, I had to run twelve rounds daily, which took me twenty-five minutes to complete. I would cool down and then do stretching exercises, followed by a physiotherapy session, where a physiotherapist checked the parts of the body that felt sore and worked on them. I would rest through the day and get ready for the sparring sessions in the evening. I paired up with different partners for two hours every day. I was keen on practicing feint attack techniques, but my coach wanted me to strengthen my body, particularly my belly. I also did circuit training, which is very tiring. If I slowed down even a little, Charles would say, 'Come on, Mary, faster.' On the other hand, when I displayed extra aggression in the ring, he'd say, 'Calm down, calm down.' When I got too aggressive, I would throw punches blindly. I needed to stay calm and make the right, calculated moves. Charles was a positive, affirmative presence in my life in the run-up to the Olympics.

When I had time to myself, I would often think back to the celebrations that marked the one-year countdown to the opening ceremony in London. We were assembled at the British High Commissioner's residence in New Delhi. An Omega Countdown Clock was to be unveiled by Abhinav Bindra, India's first individual Olympic gold medallist, and I, in my capacity as an aspirant. For a year from then, and all through my time at Pune, that clock was ticking away, counting down the days, hours, minutes and seconds to the Olympics. The thought of it only reinforced my determination to bring home a gold.

14

At the Olympics

July 2012. I was on a flight to London. For years, I had dreamt of this moment; for months, I had thought of nothing else. Yet I did not fully know what to expect. I called my husband and sons. Onler, as always, spoke words of encouragement and assurance. My sons demanded to know where I was, then commanded me to come back soon with lots of goodies. I closed my eyes and prayed. As the plane took off, I thought of Rengpa and Nainai. Deep in my heart I knew what the best gift for them would be, and resolved once again that I would do all I could to bring it home. They might not understand what it was all about but one day, when they grew up, they would. And they would understand why their mother was missing in action so often in their childhood years.

At Heathrow, I felt as if I were a matador facing an angry, rampaging bull. There were posters advertising the Games everywhere, and I could feel my stomach fluttering with excitement and anticipation.

Charles was waiting for me in Liverpool. It was a relief to

see his familiar face. We had planned on reaching early so that I could acclimatize to the British climate. While I was training, the local kids would often come to watch me. I felt buoyed by their excitement. I stayed at a Kirby Park B&B, run by Sharron and her husband, a hospitable, affectionate couple. The home-like atmosphere was much more to my liking than a hotel.

We practiced at a boxing gym Charles was familiar with. He had arranged for sparring partners for me from the gym. By this stage, I needed to be comfortable sparring with anyone at all. My intense training was not only physical. I also mentally calculated my moves according to the opponents I thought I would meet.

Charles himself had come to be a father figure to me. While his technique and skills have improved me as a boxer tremendously, it is his love that I will always carry in my heart. I am fortunate to have been able to train under him.

The days before the Olympics were devoted to training and rest. Media persons were not allowed to meet me. Even calls from my family were restricted to keep me free from stress and worry. I spent time in prayer and meditation. I told myself often: 'If God is for us, who can be against us?'

My physiotherapist, Dr Nikhil Latey, head of the OGQ sports medicine team, was with me throughout. He lifted my morale by many notches when he told me that I recovered faster from injuries than any athlete he'd come across.

A few days before the women's boxing events were to begin, I moved to the Olympic Games Village to stay with the rest of the Indian contingent. The women's boxing bouts were to be held towards the end of the Games. I tried to relax and preserve my energy, and practised a little by myself in the morning and evening. The one thing I most wished for those days was for Charles's presence but he was not allowed to stay in the Village. The chief coach of the women's boxing team, Anoop Kumar, was with me.

I had joined my team at the Village quite late. The other players were already busy with their own matches and practices. I would meet the Indian athletes in the dining hall and we would greet each other. I know Gagan Narang and Vijay Kumar a little better than the others, as they are also OGQ-sponsored athletes and I've had more opportunities to interact with them. I also took out time to talk to Devendro Singh, who is also Manipuri and a talented young boxer. When he lost, I counselled him, 'A game is a game. One wins and one loses. You are young and you have a promising career ahead of you. Don't be disheartened.' Of course, it's easier to give such advice than take it.

As part of my preparation for the Games, I had to keep checking my weight. Whenever my weight went down, I needed to eat more. This was easier said than done, because the food was too sweet for my liking. I ate a very heavy breakfast, because I preferred that menu to lunch or dinner.

A day before my first bout, my husband and mother arrived in London, leaving the twins in the care of Sempi, Onler's sister, and other relatives. Although their hotel was quite some distance from the Village, I managed to meet them. The very sight of them set my spirit soaring. Their presence did wonders for my confidence as I prepared for my first fight the following day. I was ready for action.

Before my first bout, I called father to say, 'Apa, please pray for me. I have to play today.'

He assured me, 'Don't worry, I'm always praying for you. Sanahen, I am confident you will not come back empty-handed. May God bless you abundantly.'

My first bout on 5 August was against Karolina Michalczuk of Poland. It was a special day for me – the birthday of my twins. It was an auspicious day for my inaugural entry to the Olympics. I was convinced that nothing would go wrong. So I quelled my nervousness at the vastness of the stage – this was the Olympics, after all. I regained my composure and asked myself why I needed to be afraid. My opponents, like me, would have two hands, two feet and two eyes. As before every other bout, I repeated my magic mantra: 'I must win this bout, I must win, I must win.' With that silent prayer, I turned to my opponent.

She turned out to be very strong. It was like hitting a concrete wall. Caught unawares, at one point, I lost my footing and fell. But she lacked technique. I used skill and tactics, and drew upon my experience of facing such strong but raw boxers to counter her attacks. I flung hooks at her head and emptied every bit of reserve stamina I had, but won the bout decisively: 19–4. I declared to the Indian media that had gathered there that this first win was a gift to my sons. It was the first hurdle crossed.

I was overwhelmed by the support of my fans. During the bouts, I could hear my supporters shouting, 'Mary Kom, Mary Kom'. It really set my adrenalin flowing. In the crowd, I could see Bijoy Koijam Sir and Dileep Sir, who had come all the way from Manipur. I felt indebted to the European Manipuri Association (EMA) for their support, and for the support of my compatriots – some of them lived there, others travelled from across India to be part of the greatest show on earth.

My second bout, on 6 August, against Maroua Rahali of Tunisia, was relatively easier. I started off on the defensive in the first two rounds but won them all the same. In the third round, I bounced back, going back to my bop-bop-bop style.

I'm sure Rahali was taken aback at the sudden change in pace. I won the bout 15–6.

I had reached the semi-finals. Not only was I a step closer to the finals, I was also now assured of a medal. If nothing else, I would return home with a bronze medal. Yes, I wanted gold. But at least, like my father had predicted, I wouldn't return empty-handed.

With only a day of rest, I was up against Adams on 8 August. Remember that it was Adams who had beaten me in the qualifiers. She was bigger and stronger than me, having worked her way down from a higher weight category to fight in the 51kg class.

I was wearing red, she, blue. I had played against her and knew that she had the advantage of height. Her reach was much better than mine. Being the shorter, smaller boxer, I did most of the attacking but try as I might, I could not get close enough to hit. Mentally, I was in good spirits and not afraid to face her. But physically, I wasn't in my best form. The first bout against Karolina had taken a toll on me. My body felt tight and stiff. My movements and my feet were slower than usual. I fought desperately, but she won 11–6. I was devastated but I also knew that I couldn't have tried harder, that I had left no stone unturned. I had given it my best. As far as I was concerned, I had been honest with myself. I couldn't have done more.

As I left the hall, the spectators gave me a standing ovation. I was humbled and moved; I left knowing that I would always remember these three bouts. But the curtains had come down on my Olympic run.

The moment I stepped out of the stadium, I was surrounded by journalists who started shooting questions faster than any blows I'd parried. At the best of times, I am media-shy. I had stayed away in Liverpool until my event came up, so I could avoid unwanted attention and keep calm. And now, my heart was heavy and my dreams shattered. I found it difficult to say anything. During a video conference with Prakash Padukone and Geet Sethi, live on TV, I was overcome with sorrow and remorse. 'I am sorry I could not win gold,' I told them, but also my countrymen and women.

I really was sorry. After all the effort that had been expended on me, I felt I owed the country more than a bronze.

I called my father and broke down on the phone. He was quiet for a while, then said, 'Look, my daughter, the gold is not your birthright. God gave you what you deserve. I am very happy you got an Olympic medal. Don't be discouraged. There will be other times. Be thankful for what you got.'

My coach, Charles, seconded that. His words too meant a lot to me. He told the media later, 'I've watched that match several times, and I can honestly say that Mary was the better fighter. Adams won because she fought defensively and did not pick a physical fight. Mary played the eventual gold medallist and didn't get a scratch on her.' This was balm to my soul.

Standing on the podium for the medal ceremony, my heart was burning, almost bursting with pain. How I yearned for the gold and for the Indian national anthem to be played. I tried to smile for all the world to see, but couldn't help feeling that I had let down my country. But again I consoled myself thinking that I would try again the next time.

The fact is that it took me days to realize that I was now an Olympic medallist – every sportsperson's dream. Suddenly, it felt like all the media attention was on me. It was more than I had expected or imagined possible.

After the Olympics, the EMA and its general secretary, Somorendro Khangembam, had organized a special meet at a London pub. Many Manipuris came to meet and greet me, and congratulate me for putting our state on the world map. My association with EMA continues. One of its members recently sent me $1,000 for my academy in memory of his grandparents.

After I had attended a few more official engagements, I returned to India with Onler and Anu. On the flight I thought of the many times I had walked out, leaving my sons behind, holding my chin up. My relatives, watching with tears in their eyes, would not have suspected that my heart was breaking too. It was worth the sacrifice, though, for I was returning with an Olympic medal. Some day, my boys will be old enough to understand, and I hope they will be proud of me.

15

What came after

The plane touched down in the wee hours of the morning. It was still dark in Delhi. By the time we completed our paperwork and stepped into the arrivals lounge, the sun had begun to rise. All of a sudden, I found myself surrounded by guards who ushered me along without saying where they were taking me. And where were Onler and mother? No one would answer me.

Then I stepped outside the airport and understood. A huge crowd welcomed me with bands playing music and everyone trying to garland me. It was a rousing, overwhelming, emotional welcome. I tried looking for my family but the IABF had organized a vehicle into which I was quickly guided, and we started to leave the airport terminal. We were slowed down by the media, who wanted to interview me, and so managed to only inch forward.

By the time we had done a hundred metres or so, I was frantic. I wanted desperately to see my children, who had come to the airport. I felt lost and alone in that crowd. I put my foot down and threatened to jump off the moving vehicle if they didn't let me meet my family. Only then did the vehicle turn around and take me back to the airport. There, I found some Kom students who helped me locate my children and family. My sons saw me and ran up, beaming. I hugged them – at that moment, I didn't care about anything else.

Seeing that this was their chance, the girls and boys who had helped me find my family earlier, welcomed me with drums and gongs and our traditional dance. I happily joined in. It felt like a proper homecoming. My family and I then left for Ashoka Hotel, where the Sports Ministry had arranged for us to stay.

With the request that the media allow me a few hours break, I finally rested for a while. The next few days were an endless schedule of felicitation programmes and events to celebrate my achievement. I finally left for Imphal after about four days in Delhi.

Devendro and I travelled to Imphal on the same flight. When we landed, we were greeted by a massive crowd. The sounds of drums filled the air. In the arrivals lounge, I was welcomed with a traditional sarong and shawl. There was a flower-bedecked open jeep outside for the victory ride across Imphal town. The near-constant rain and drizzle did nothing to dampen the spirits of those gathered. I heard shouts of 'Long live Mary Kom' and 'Long live Devendro', and saw garlands and flowers being tossed in the air toward us. Once again, a reception had been organized at Khuman Lampak Sports Complex, with the chief minister and other ministers, the four state Olympians – Laishram Bombayla Devi, Ng Soniya Chanu, Devendro and I – as well as the boxing community and many others in attendance. I received a cheque of Rs 75 lakh and the others Rs 20 lakh each from Ibobi Singh. 'Today is the happiest day of my life, as I have returned to Ima [mother] Manipur after bagging a medal at the London Olympics and that has always been my dream,' I said to those gathered.

The government announced that it would promote me to the rank of Superintendent of Police (Sports) and allotted me three acres of land to run the M.C. Mary Kom Boxing Academy. My earlier promotion – after the fifth World Championship gold – had not yet materialized, but the Olympic bronze helped this one come through quickly. The paperwork for the allotment of land for the Academy has also been finally completed. The Academy will allow me to share with the next generation of boxers my passion for the sport. I want to give them the platform that I had to fight for, and nurture their talent.

I believe with all my heart that if you pursue your dream with all the zeal at your command, nothing is impossible. I dared to dream big in spite of my humble beginnings. I hope that my life is proof to youngsters across India that it is possible to do more if they dare, if they have the will.

16

My tryst with glamour

The fame and fortune that came with the Olympic medal has been beyond anything my family or I imagined possible. I've met unapproachable people, and realized that they are normal people like you and I. Sanjay Dutt, Aamir Khan, Deepika Padukone, Priyanka Chopra, Shilpa Shetty and Raj Kundra impressed me with their simplicity and friendship. I met so many sportspeople and found common ground with them. Saina Nehwal, Sushil Kumar, Yogeshwar Dutt, Vijay Kumar, Gagan Narang, they were all wonderful. I grew particularly fond of Gagan, who treats me like an elder sister.

One time, as part of a fund-raising charity fashion show that actress Shabana Azmi and other celebrities had organized in Mumbai, I was asked to walk the ramp. Also part of the show were industrialists and various film personalities. In the green room, I was dressed in a pink designer outfit designed by Manish Malhotra. I was terribly nervous, of course, but as soon as I walked on stage, the audience stood up to applaud me – it was as if they knew I was nervous and could do with the help. I felt very pretty in that gorgeous dress, like someone out of a fairy tale. I let go of my inhibitions and enjoyed myself. The crowd went wild.

Posing for photo shoots, cutting ribbons, accepting prizes and awards – those I could do. But when it came to attending talk shows and giving speeches, I got nervous and tongue-tied. I am still like that. Except for a fortunate few, sportspeople tend to be uncomfortable with public speaking. I joked and shared my experiences with others who were even worse off than me; it was good to know that I wasn't alone. Gagan, I noticed, always has a slip of paper in his hand. Among the Olympians, Vijay Kumar seems to be the only one quite at ease with public speaking. The rest say they feel awkward when asked to make public speeches.

One of the more challenging and heartening aspects of my new profile was giving motivational talks to students. They asked me many questions about my early life, how I balanced my professional and personal lives and, naturally, about boxing. In one school, the students asked me to sing for them. I obliged with a Hindi song. It was heartening for me to see a few students from Manipur everywhere I went. I was glad that youngsters from my remote state were out in other cities and getting the best education our country has to offer, getting the opportunities they wouldn't get in Manipur.

The other new experience in my life was doing photo shoots. I had always imagined that a shoot would take barely a few minutes. How innocent I was. It took a whole day for me to shoot for an advertisement in Mumbai. Putting on make-up, changing clothes, the shoot itself – I had no idea there was so much hard work and so many people involved. Poor Onler too had to wait patiently while I went through the ordeal of putting on those layers of make-up. At the end of it, he joked,

'Anyone will look good after such a long make-up session.' But I think he was pleased by the transformation.

My favourite photo shoot was for the one with the caption 'Our Kom-mitment to the Nation'. The billboards seem to be in every nook and corner of Imphal and elsewhere in the Northeast. Every time I see it, I am reminded of how far I've come, and how far we can all come if we feel strongly enough about something and work hard enough.

I am not choosy about my commercial endorsements, but I decline offers that would spoil my image or promote something I am uncomfortable with, even if they offer more money. On the other hand, there are projects I am willing to take on that have nothing to do with the money. I was particularly happy to be the brand ambassador for the Super Fight League.

The travel that accompanied all this glamour was tiring. There were times when I was in two cities on the same day to fulfil commitments. Home seemed more distant than ever. I don't know how I would have managed if Onler had not been by my side. That he was there made the travel as pleasant as it could be.

The most difficult part of all this is that I am not home enough. My friends say, 'Mary, you must be tired. You and your family should go on a holiday.' My favourite holiday destination is quite simply my home. It's humble and messy, but there's no place I'd rather be.

The moment I step into the house, I shed the sports celebrity skin and take over the running of the house – usually with the children clinging to me, because they don't see me enough. I do try to be back as often as I can. Sometimes I come back even if it's only for a day or two, rather than rest elsewhere. As soon as I'm back, I check if everything's in order with the kids: their clothes, books, shoes, toys and so on.

I then move on to putting my house in order. I clean the compound, backyard and every nook and corner with the help of the nephews, nieces and cousins who are staying with me just then. I rearrange things around the house, and only then do I sit back and relax. Not for long though, because my husband and children have been waiting for me to come home and cook for them. I enjoy cooking and I've been told that I'm good at it. I often cook for the students of the Academy; they compliment me by finishing every last grain of rice there is. Needless to say, I cook all the dishes I missed while I was away. For me, the choicest five-star food does not compare to simple home-cooked meals.

For Onler, the best part of my presence at home probably is that he can catch up on his sleep. He has more time to spare and to catch up with work and deadlines. He is happy and relaxed when I'm around. For one, I take the children off his hands. Ironing their clothes, sticking labels on their books, helping with their homework – in the little time I have with my boys, I want to do it all.

I love doing the simple things in life. Gardening, for instance. I spend my free time planting vegetables in the backyard. I love to see the plants grow. One morning, I woke up to find that our two dogs had made a complete mess of a sapling. I was furious. I made a tight fence around the garden so they couldn't get to it.

My professional life spills over into the home as well, of course. Many journalists and photographers visit me. Often I am in the middle of washing clothes or dishes, or cooking a special dish for the family, when they come. I have to keep them waiting, because I cannot leave things half done. At such times, Onler meets them and talks to them, giving me time to wrap things up. He helps me with my speeches and with the things I want to say.

My extended family lives with me, including my brother-in-law's four children. Their father, James, nicknamed James Bond by the family, was a football player in his youth. James's son, Oneithang, is one of the most promising boxers at the Academy. My niece Tonijoy is heaven-sent. She has been caring for my twins with so much love that it has to be seen. My sister-in-law, Sempi, who lives nearby, also chips in with looking after the twins. Needless to say, my mother is deeply involved with the care of her grandchildren. Raising my sons has been a joint family endeavour.

It is a comforting thought that I can leave my children in safe hands when I am away. But in the midst of my photo shoots and felicitation ceremonies, I can never put my worries completely at rest. Onler is not adept at housekeeping and the others are too young to run a house well. I am fortunate that my relatives all come by and keep things in working order. But for them, the boxing gloves would be hanging somewhere, gathering dust. When the celebrations have wound up and the fame is gone, I know I have my family to come home to.

I suspect that Onler may want me to come home sooner rather than later. After the Olympics, at the felicitation function organized by the Kom-Rem Fellowship in Imphal, I spoke about my desire to work hard for the Rio de Janeiro Olympic Games in 2016. Onler said, only half in jest, that it's extremely hard to raise two young boys and manage a home without a wife, and so I should consider hanging up my gloves. We are yet to negotiate that.

Meanwhile, it is a matter of pride and joy to me that Anu and Apa are finally in a good place in their lives. They continue to stay in Kangathei, because they like living in the village with friends and relatives around. I've asked them but they don't want to shift to town. Their house has been transformed, though, with the rooms they have added to it. They now use cooking gas in the kitchen. A two-wheel tractor has replaced the bullocks. The granary is filled with rice for a year. My sister is married and now has a daughter. She lives in Kohima, Nagaland and keeps a lovely home. My brother too is married and our parents will soon be doting grandparents to more children. Apa and Anu are happy and contented.

I know for a fact that fame hasn't changed me very much. I am still shy in public, yet aggressive in the ring. I am as short-tempered as I always was, and just as loving. My life still revolves around my family and boxing. What's changed is that I can now afford luxuries: I own a house (more than one actually, thanks to two corporate gifts), two cars and I travel by air when I need to. I used to dream about a BMW but now that I can afford one, I think it's too expensive and the roads in my hometown are not ideal for such expensive cars.

I was also able to finally fulfil the promise I made to Anu. In December 2012, I handed over the keys of a Bolero to my father. While Anu touched it shyly, Apa checked every part of the car as if he were an expert mechanic. He sat behind the wheel promptly, although he doesn't know how to drive. He looked so tiny behind the wheel that I said, 'Apa, it will look better if Anu drives and you sit next to her.' Everyone burst out laughing. Eventually, we had to hire a driver to take the vehicle home. As they sat in the car, laughing and joking, my heart filled with their joy at the gift. Every time Apa looks at the Bolero, he will know that our years of struggle were not in vain.

If I haven't changed after all the success I've had, neither have my parents. They are still the simple village folk who farm for a living. Only, Apa has become an expert at speaking to the media. He does most of the talking, seeking Anu's help only when he's confused about some event in my life.

Film-maker Sanjay Leela Bhansali is actually making a movie based on my life. Blue Lotus Productions contacted Jimmy, who handles my professional life, sometime in early 2011. They said they were interested in my story and that it would make for a good movie. I met them in Imphal with Onler, Jimmy and a couple of other friends and advisors, and we all felt comfortable working with each other. I would never have thought anything about my life was so interesting, but I hope that it is a source of inspiration to children across India. I'm pleased, of course, that someone as beautiful and talented as Priyanka Chopra should be playing me.

Just when things quietened down a little, I was nominated for the Padma Bhushan. For once, I didn't think I deserved it, because I managed to get only a bronze. The silver medallists, Vijay Kumar and Sushil Kumar, deserved it more. It was deeply humbling, and filled me with renewed energy and passion to do more for my country and my sport.

The aftermath of fame hasn't always been easy to handle. There is a general opinion that I rake in millions, and I cope with that every day I am home. I get countless requests for donations for all sorts of causes. Some of these are good causes that I know to be genuine. Others, I have no way of finding out. And I certainly do not have the wherewithal to accede to every request I get. I have also read too many stories of famous sportspeople dying in penury to spend incautiously right now. I wasn't born with a silver spoon in my mouth. It's hard for me to believe that all of this will last.

But I do want to give back to sport and society, and I do that through the M.C. Mary Kom Boxing Academy. I also want to be a champion of hope for the women of my country. I want them to look at me and see their image in me. I want them to believe that if I can make it, so can they.

17

My vision for the future

I have been vocal in my demand for the upliftment of sports other than cricket, in spite of the hostility I faced for that stance. For a large part of my career, I had no sponsors. I have even, on occasion, paid for my travel to participate in competitions and camps. I have proven that women can achieve as much as men can, and I have shown that boxing can be as engrossing as cricket for Indians. Today, there is a marked improvement in facilities for other sports. I hope that my academy will prove to be another step towards bringing boxing out of the sidelines, and providing both boys and girls with the encouragement they need to excel.

I run the M.C. Mary Kom Boxing Academy absolutely free of charge. It focuses on underprivileged children. My own experiences have taught me how difficult it is to follow one's dream without any support or resources. Many youths in the far-flung villages of my state drop out of school and then, with no means to earn a livelihood, join the insurgency. Others marry early and end up with a big family, continuing the cycle of poverty. Yet others, with no one to guide them, resort to drugs as a means to escape reality. I hope the Academy will channel the energy and frustration of at least some of those youths to the noble art of boxing.

I established the Academy in my backyard with very few resources in 2006, with a clear vision: quality boxers with potential from the underprivileged class. When we began, we had no proper infrastructure, or even a boxing ring. All I was armed with was talent, experience and the support of my husband. To date, we function without a permanent address or a proper hostel for the students. But now that land has finally been allocated, I am hopeful that we will have a roof over our heads sometime in the not-so-distant future.

The idea for a boxing academy was born on a trip to Mokokching village for a function in 2005. There, I happened to meet my sister-in-law's younger sister, Nengneihat. When I saw her, it struck me that she could have potential as a boxer – her height, build, boyish appearance, all of it appealed to me. She was an orphan, staying with her relatives. I sought the permission of her elders, brought her home with me and began to teach her the basics of boxing. She was the first of my extended family to join us; the number gradually increased over the years. Nengneihat was a fast learner, and soon became my sparring partner at home during my daily practice.

When the news spread that I was teaching a student, many parents started bringing their children to me, with a request that I teach them boxing. Unable to refuse, I began to teach a few of them. The number of students gradually increased. Then Onler came up with the idea of a boxing academy. I was already so busy that the idea didn't appeal to me in the beginning. I was happy to teach children, but managing an institution seemed like too much trouble. But Onler explained to me that a formalized academy would be the best and most organized way to impart my knowledge to a new generation of boxers, and it would allow me to take in more students too. When I thought about it in that light, the idea appealed to me greatly.

Although I did not possess a coaching diploma, I felt that my years of training and experience would suffice for teaching students the basics of boxing.

So, in addition to the students whose parents brought them to me, I scouted for youngsters from poor families who appeared to have potential. Some of my boys and girls are as young as ten, but most are in their teens. The expenses – food, lodging, an extra coach, a warden for the students – came from my pocket. Most months, it was my entire pay packet. My efforts paid off when my first student, Nengneihat, began to win medals. In 2008, she won gold at the All India Inter-SAI, followed by silver the next year. At the national level, she managed to get a silver and bronze, and at the state level, she won two golds.

Only after my students started getting medals did the Academy come to be recognized. Ten of our boxers have been referred to the SAI centre in Khuman Lampak. T.S. Merina Chiru won a gold at the Second National Women's Sub-Junior Boxing Championships in 2011. K. Oneithang Kom is another promising boxer, who has won gold at the state level, followed by a silver. OGQ is sponsoring Nengneihat and Oneithang as medal potentials, which in itself is a great achievement for the Academy.

In 2010, the Academy was renamed 'M.C. Mary Kom Regional Boxing Foundation' after it was upgraded to a regional academy – that is, it is now officially recognized and is meant to cater to all of the Northeast. But we are still functioning without proper facilities and infrastructure. The workout and sparring is done in the open every morning and afternoon. Onler and I worry about this, because our training must necessarily stop during the monsoons. There are no rings, no proper rooms to house the equipment and a rented house serves as hostel for the students. I make arrangements for the boys and girls to live separately. Some of the students also stay in my house when the rented accommodation is not enough, until such time that we can arrange a place for them to stay. Most of them are from far-off villages, so accommodation is a big issue for us.

Slowly, things are falling into place. The army – which has a very lively culture of boxing – has been actively supporting my academy with donations of a generator, boxing gear, gymnasium and even kitchen equipment. As I was writing this book, the allotment of the two-acre land, which Chief Minister O. Ibobi Singh promised me, has come through. Under the SAI extension scheme, SAI Manipur has been providing sports kits and a stipend of Rs 600 per month for my students since August 2010.

The student strength keeps fluctuating. Some students drop out because of health reasons, others are asked to leave. It is of utmost importance that a sportsperson should be disciplined, obedient and hard-working. As of mid-2013, there are thirty-four students, of whom ten are not boarders.

The students are like members of my extended family. In addition to sports training, I spend time exhorting them to work hard. I tell them about my life, and hope that it will inspire them. 'Look at me. I am a nobody who became a sporting icon only because of my consistent hard work,' I say. I teach them to be modest, but to aim big. I don't hesitate to point out their mistakes and correct them. I am a very strict teacher when I'm coaching. But I'm an equally affectionate mentor. I often tell them, 'You are fortunate to have a world champion as your cook.'

When I look at these kids, I think back on my own life. I hope that boxing opens their minds and hearts as it did mine. Over these years, I have made close friends, of whom Jenny is the one I am most in touch with. The girls and I spent a lot of time together, doing non-work things, especially when we went abroad. We would go out shopping. We snacked at various food stalls and tasted all sorts of foods. In India, during the off days in our training camps, we went out to watch movies. Abroad, we were taken sight-seeing, which was always fun in a group. I really enjoyed my visit to Rome. The city was beautiful and the churches divine; I'd gladly visit it again – this time with my family. Through my travels across India and my interaction with boxers from across the country, I learnt about the different cultures of India and what it means to be truly Indian. All of this and more I wish for the youngsters at my academy.

The official coach of the Academy is S. Naobi Singh from Sekta, Imphal. I join him to teach students the finer tactics of sparring. Onler fills in to guide students on their exercises whenever he can spare the time. Nengneihat is a sort of monitor for the rest, because she is the most experienced of the lot.

It is my dream to make this an international-standard boxing academy with excellent facilities. It will be a place where children can train and study free of cost and bring in medals for the country. I hope that sometime in the future we will be able to extend our facilities to include education, so that there is all-round development of the sportspeople we train.

Violent crimes against women are on the rise in India – a phenomenon that I have been observing with alarm. I have been considering adapting my training in boxing to self-defence courses. Perhaps I can provide such courses for women, and not just in Manipur, in the future.

A country like India has a lot of potential. I end with the hope that we will build on that. My life is my message: nothing is impossible.

Afterword

After the Olympics, in the blur of award functions, non-stop travel, photo shoots, talk shows and interviews, I failed to notice the symptoms of something quite vital. I was pregnant again. The nausea and tiredness could so easily have been due to the crazy schedule I was keeping. It was only in mid-November 2012, when I was travelling by road, that I felt particularly out of sorts. I began to suspect that I needed a medical check-up. Once I got home, I arranged for this immediately and the results came back positive for pregnancy. I was three months pregnant, I learnt.

This time too, I had no plans for a baby. But I took the news gladly, accepting it as yet another blessing from God. I cut down on my commitments and took much-needed rest at home. By then, I had begun work on my autobiography. One of the reasons you're holding this book in your hands is that my pregnancy forced a break in my normal schedule, giving me time to think and reflect on the past, to look forward to the future.

My third child was born on 13 May 2013. Once again, it was a C-section. The doctors said that the baby would be big and that a normal delivery would be risky. I was hoping for a daughter after my two boys. But the child was a boy. The healthy baby boy – 3.8 kg at birth – was cause for huge celebrations at home. My sons were delighted to have a baby brother and took turns holding him. We were worried that they would smother the newborn with their hugs and kisses.

This time, my husband had already decided that my grandmother – Chungthem, the eldest in our family, and almost a hundred years old now – would name him. She had also named me. Onler felt that it would be an honour to have a son named by her. She came up with a few names, but finally decided on Chungthanglen, which means height, fame and largeness, because he was born at the height of my sporting glory. The name Grandmother bestowed on him also called down a blessing on him: that he be endowed with fame, attain great heights and become a large-hearted, good person.

Not satisfied with one name, I wanted a nickname for him. My sons wanted 'Prince Son', and I opted for Prince, since both the families are descendants of chiefs.

Chungthanglen Prince – my third son – is an added joy to the family. As I watch him grow, I am also waiting for the months to pass, so I can start my fitness exercises and pick up my boxing gloves. Rio 2016 is round the corner, you see.

Annexures

Annexure 1:
Medals

National Achievements

	Tournament/championship	*Dates*	*Result*
1.	7th East Open Boxing Championship, Bengal	11–14 Dec 2000	Gold
2.	1st Women's National Boxing Championship, Chennai	6–11 Feb 2001	Gold
3.	2nd Senior Women's National Boxing Championship, New Delhi	26–30 Dec 2001	Gold
4.	32nd National Games, Hyderabad	13–22 Dec 2002	Gold
5.	National Women's Sports Meet, New Delhi	26–30 Dec 2002	Gold
6.	3rd Senior Women's National Boxing Championship, Aizawl	4–8 Mar 2003	Gold
7.	4th Senior Women's National Boxing Championship, Assam	24–28 Feb 2004	Gold

	Tournament/championship	Dates	Result
8.	5th Senior Women's National Boxing Championship, Kerala	26–30 Dec 2004	Gold
9.	6th National Senior Women's Boxing Championship, Jamshedpur	29 Nov–3 Dec 2005	Gold
10.	9th Senior Women's National Boxing Championship, Agra	2–7 Nov 2008	Gold
11.	57th All India Police Meet, Pune	6–10 Apr 2010	Gold
12.	12th Senior National Women's Boxing Championship, Bhopal	11–16 Oct 2011	Gold

International Achievements

	Tournament/championship	Dates	Result
1.	1st World Women's Boxing Championship, 45 kg, Pennsylvania, USA	27 Nov–2 Dec 2001	Silver
2.	Witch Cup Boxing Championship, Paes, Hungary, 45 kg	27–31 Aug 2002	Gold
3.	2nd World Women's Boxing Championship, Antalya, Turkey	19–28 Oct 2002	Gold
4.	Training-cum-competition, Rome, Italy	2–13 Sept 2003	3 Golds

	Tournament/championship	Dates	Result
5.	2nd Asian Women's Boxing Championship, Hisar, India	19–22 Nov 2003	Gold
6.	1st World Women's Boxing Tournament, Tonsberg, Norway, 46 kg	27 Apr–2 May 2004	Gold
7.	3rd Asian Women's Boxing Championship, Taiwan, 46 kg	5–12 Aug 2005	Gold
8.	Asian Cadet Boxing Championship, Hanoi, Vietnam, 46 kg	10–18 June 2006	Gold
9.	4th World Women's Boxing Championship, New Delhi, India, 46 kg	17–24 Nov 2006	Gold
10.	Vijle Women's Boxing Tournament, Denmark	18–23 Oct 2006	Gold
11.	4th Asian Women's Boxing Championship, Guwahati, India, 46 kg	23–7 Sept 2008	Silver
12.	5th World Women's Boxing Championship, Ningbo, China, 46 kg	22–29 Nov 2008	Gold
13.	Indo-Sweden Dual Match Boxing Tournament, Gothenberg, Sweden	21 Mar 2009	Gold
14.	Indoor Asian Games, Hanoi, Vietnam	30 Oct–7 Nov 2009	Gold
15.	5th Asian Women's Boxing Championship, Astana, Kazakhstan, 51 kg	23–30 May 2010	Gold

	Tournament/championship	Dates	Result
16.	6th AIBA Women's World Boxing Championship, Barbados, 48 kg	7–18 Sept 2010	Gold
17.	16th Asian Games, Guangzhou, China, 51 kg	12–28 Dec,2010	Bronze
18.	Asia Cup, Haikou, China, 48 kg	5–9 May 2011	Gold
19.	6th Asian Women's Boxing Championship, Mongolia. 51 kg	16–26 Mar 2012	Gold
20.	Olympic Games 2012, London, 51 kg	27 July–12 Aug 2012	Bronze

Other Championships

	Tournament/Championship	Year	Medal
1.	1st Asian Women's Boxing Championship, Bangkok, Thailand	2001	Lost
2.	Training at Pyongyang, North Korea	25 Sept–24 Oct 2004	
3.	7th AIBA, Women World Boxing Championship (also Olympic Qualifier), Qinhuangdao, China	9 May–22 May 2012	Lost, but qualified for Olympics

Annexure 2:
Awards

1. Arjuna Award, 2003 (21 September 2004)
2. Padma Shri Award, 2005 (20 March 2006)
3. NETV People's Choice Awards, 2006
4. People of the Year, 2007, Limca Book of Records: India at her best
5. Indian Real Heroes Award, 2007, CNN-IBN, Reliance Industries Limited, Mumbai
6. Pepsi MTV Youth Icon, 2008
7. Param Poojaniya Shri Guruji Puruskar, 2009, RSS Jankalyan, Maharashtra Prant
8. Rajiv Gandhi Khel Ratna Award, 2009 (29 August 2009)
9. North East Excellence Award, 2009 (8–9 January 2010)
10. Sports Women of the year 2008–09, Sahara India Parivar
11. YFLO Women Achiever 2009–10, FICCI Ladies Organization
12. Sportsperson of the Year, North East, 2010, Assam Sports Journalist Association
13. Sports Women of the Year, 2010–11, Sahara India Parivar
14. Spirit of Sports Award, 2012, NDTV India, 5 March 2012
15. Tribal Achiever's Award, 2012, Ministry of Tribal Affairs, Government of India
16. Padma Bhushan, 2013 (20 April 2013)

Annexure 3:
Letters of appreciation

Pranab Mukherjee
President, Republic of India

9 August 2012

I am extremely delighted to know that you have won the Bronze Medal in Women's Boxing in the fly weight 51 kg at the London Olympics. This is a great achievement and should inspire women as well as sportspersons throughout the nation.

I would like to extend my congratulations and best wishes for further success in the future.

Pratibha Devisingh Patil
President, Republic of India

24 September 2010

I am extremely delighted to know that you have clinched the Women's World Boxing Championship for the fifth consecutive time. This is a great achievement and should inspire women sportspersons throughout the nation.

Sonia Gandhi
Chairperson, United Progressive Alliance

13 August 2012

My warmest congratulations to you for your brilliant performance at the 2012 Olympics! Your Bronze Medal in women's boxing has brought honour and glory to our country, and thrilled the hearts of all Indians.

Your steadfast dedication, discipline and indomitable courage are a source of inspiration to all of us. Every Indian, every Manipuri and indeed every woman takes immense pride in your achievements. I am confident you will continue to win laurels for India in the future, and come back with a Gold in the next Olympics!

I hope you are enjoying a happy reunion with your family and your adorable twin sons, and taking a well-deserved rest now.

Abhay Singh Chautala
Member of Legislative Assembly and President, Indian Olympic Association

5 February 2013

I heartily congratulate you on being nominated for the prestigious Padma Bhushan Puraskar for 2013.

You are great source of inspiration to the budding sportspersons of the country.

I am confident that you will bring more laurels to the country in future.

Suresh Kalmadi
Member of Parliament and President, Indian Olympic Association

27 January 2006

Heartiest congratulations on being conferred the prestigious Padma Shri award for your contribution to sport. This is indeed a well-deserved recognition considering your sterling achievements in your chosen discipline.

You have set high standards and enhanced the prestige of the nation. I am sure this award will encourage you to continue in the future, inspire others to follow in your footsteps and take Indian sport to new heights.

General J.J. Singh
PVSM, AVSM, VSM (Retd), Governor, Arunachal Pradesh

31 July 2009

It was a great pleasure to see your name in the country's highest sporting honour's list, for being conferred with the Rajiv Gandhi Khel Ratna Award this year for your outstanding performance in boxing. This recognition of your excellence in boxing is indeed a matter of pride for all of us, and it will be a source of inspiration for the youth of the country.

Meenaxi Anand Chaudhry
Secretary, Ministry of Youth Affairs and Sports

28 September 2004

Congratulations once again on your winning the coveted Arjuna Award! I have no doubt that this recognition by the Government will spur you to achieve greater laurels for the country. As crores of young men and women look up to you for inspiration, I hope that you will be willing to do your humble bit for the welfare of the society by raising your voice against social evils and lending your weight behind socially relevant causes.

Annexure 4:
A word about my sponsors

My sporting journey has been a success story due to the contribution of my sponsors, all of whom responded to my plea for recognition and appreciation.

I am thankful to my first corporate sponsor, Raj Kumar Markan, chairman and managing director of Thermex QST Rebars, H&K India, who in 2006 made me the Brand Ambassador of Thermex for two years and provided me with much-needed financial help. The additional sponsorship of Arzoo.com in 2007 enabled me to travel by air to get better training facilities, for which I remain grateful.

Since 2009, Infinity Optimal Solutions (IOS) has managed my sporting career and enabled me to get the best facilities available for training to realize my Olympic dream.

I am thankful to Herbal Life for making me their Brand Ambassador in July 2010, and providing me with the best possible nutrition through their products. They also provide nutrition for the underprivileged students of my academy.

Cheers to Olympic Gold Quest whose wholehearted support and contribution helped me to bridge the gap between the best athletes in India and the best in the world and landed me a place on the Olympic podium.

Thank you, Monnet Ispat & Energy Limited, led by Sandeep Jajodia, who are the official sponsors of the Indian boxing team, for providing the official kit of the team. And thank you, RK Global, for supporting my personal sporting endeavour.

The immense contribution of the Army towards my academy is praiseworthy. The Army's encouragement of sports and their overwhelming support continue to inspire me. I remain thankful to them.

Annexure 5:
Favourite Bible verses

These verses from the Bible have been my source of mental strength through all the challenges in my career. In moments of weakness, my faith is renewed. Reading the Bible reassures me even in moments of stress and grief. It has encouraged and helped me to be the champion that I am today.

Matthew 11:28
Come to me, all you who are weary and burdened, and I will give you rest.

Romans 8:31
If God is for us, who can be against us?

1 Corinthians 9:24
Do you not know that in a race all the runners run, but only one gets the prize? Run in such a way as to get the prize.

Acknowledgements

For lifting me up to great heights, I thank and praise my Lord and Saviour Jesus Christ, the source of all blessings.

To my beloved husband, Onler, who, true to his promise, has stood by me at all times. His tireless efforts and support, bearing with me through all my ups and downs – for all this and more, I will always be grateful. My dear sons, Rengchungvar and Khupneivar, who have been my driving force, boosting me silently in my endeavour to reach the top. My youngest son, Chunglenthang Prince, my latest inspiration.

My due respect and thanks to my coaches and mentors for their inputs and blessings.

To all my family members, for their unfailing love and help, taking care of my home and children in my repeated absence. I will always remain grateful.

To all my beloved friends, even though I am not able to write all your names, your friendship and support helped me to strive and achieve so much.

My gratitude to all my kin and kindred, my people and my tribe, for your prayers and encouragement.

To all my fans in Manipur, India and the world, thank you so much for your best wishes and prayers at all times, particularly during competitions.

To Jimmy Leivon, for making my professional life easy, with his constant presence and handling of my work.

This book would not have been possible without the effort of a dear family friend, Dina Serto. Thank you, Au Dina, for helping me write the story of my life.

Sincere thanks to my editor, Ajitha, and HarperCollins India for publishing a book about my life, another dream come true.